KINDLE FIRE
OWNER'S MANUAL

The ultimate Kindle Fire guide to getting started, advanced user tips, and finding unlimited free books, videos and apps on Amazon and beyond

By Steve Weber

Published by Stephen W. Weber
Printed in the United States of America
Weber Books   www.WeberBooks.com
ISBN: 978-1-936560-11-0

About the author:

Steve Weber has been writing about Amazon.com for a decade.

Steve is the founder of KindleBuffet.com, a website and newsletter that displays outstanding Kindle books being offered free for a limited time.

The site also has bestseller lists of free Kindle books for every Amazon category—fiction, romance, business, cookbooks—you name it.

If you'd like to fill your Kindle bookshelf with great reading material absolutely free, visit KindleBuffet.com.

More by Steve Weber

 *eBay 101: Selling on eBay For Part-time or Full-time Income*

 Barcode Booty: How I found and sold $2 million of 'junk' on eBay and Amazon, And you can, too, using your phone

 The Home-Based Bookstore: Start Your Own Business Selling Used Books on Amazon, eBay or Your Own Web Site

Contents

Introduction

Amazon's Kindle Fire is a very affordable tablet computer. It runs on the Android operating system and, because of that, there is a wide variety of applications—called "apps"—available for it that expand its potential enormously.

Kindle Fire has a touch-screen interface, which means that there's no bulky keyboard or mouse to fuss with. The device has a brilliant, full-color seven-inch display, and serves as a fine e-reader, video or music player, web-surfing tool, game machine, and much more. Kindle Fire offers enormous utility for a low price.

Versus E-ink readers

E-ink readers use a particulate substance to form letters that are almost identical—some say even nicer to look at—than real ink on paper. Kindle Fire uses pixels, just like a regular computer screen. E-ink is currently only black and white; with the Kindle Fire you get glorious full color. This makes the Kindle Fire more suitable for multimedia use and for reading full-color publications.

Versus tablet computers

The iPad is what most people think of first when it comes to tablet computers. But compared to the Kindle Fire, the iPad has some real disadvantages.

Its hefty price is the first issue most people have with iPads. They're quite expensive and, even though they have more bells and whistles than a Kindle Fire, lots of people don't think the extra features—like a camera—are worth hundreds of dollars more.

Kindle Fire has a default interface that makes it very Amazon-centric, but we'll learn how to expand its horizon. In fact, your Amazon Kindle Fire can do just about anything that any other device running Android can do, and that's a lot. If you have an Android phone, adapting to the Kindle Fire should be quite easy.

The Kindle Fire is equipped with a dual-core processor, giving it plenty of speed. And while it does have some limitations, the Kindle Fire also has a lot to offer. A big part of Kindle's value equation is Amazon Prime.

Amazon Prime

You'll get a free month of membership to Amazon Prime with your Amazon Kindle Fire purchase. This gives you access to some pretty impressive features.

First, Amazon Prime gives you access to a large library of free instant-streaming movies and television shows. It's similar to the Netflix steaming video service, although Amazon's video library isn't as large—

yet. If you choose not to renew your Prime membership, you'll still be able to purchase movies and TV shows from Amazon in the normal fashion.

Second, Prime allows you to borrow Kindle eBooks for free. These come from the Kindle Lending Library, which is included in your Prime membership. Not all books are included in the Lending Library, but many popular books are. If you're an avid reader, the Kindle Lending Library will pay off for you quite handsomely.

Third, Prime gives you a big shipping discount when you order physical products from Amazon. You'll get free two-day delivery of many items—and overnight shipping for only $3.99—on any Prime Eligible item.

Your Prime membership will not renew unless you specifically choose to renew it, so don't worry about surprise fees. If you do choose to renew it, however, you'll get more bang out of your Kindle bucks, especially where movies and TV shows are concerned.

Your head in the Cloud Drive

You might not have heard about it yet, but as an Amazon customer you have access to a wireless storage system called "Amazon Cloud Drive." It works like a remote personal hard drive, and it really comes in handy when you have a device like the Kindle Fire. You can use it to store and back up your music, video, photos and other documents on Amazon's secure servers.

Your Cloud Drive comes with 5 gigabytes of free storage, which is enough to hold about 1,000 songs. If you need more storage space, you can get it for a monthly fee.

One important detail: the digital content you buy from Amazon—music, video and eBooks—don't count against your 5-GB limit. Your purchases are always backed up and available free in the Cloud.

1 ▶ FAST START GUIDE TO KINDLE FIRE

The Kindle Fire is an advanced eReader with extensive multimedia capabilities. The device utilizes a touch-screen for an input device. It has a 1/8" headphone/speaker jack on the bottom of the device. The wall charger port doubles as a USB connection to your computer.

If you're familiar with Kindle devices or tablet computers already, the setup process will be easy for you. Verify that your packaging contains your Kindle Fire and a wall socket charger. Remove the device from the plastic cover, plug the appropriate end of the charger cord into the Kindle, and the other end into the wall socket. Charging should take between 3 and 4 hours to complete fully, though this may vary. The light next to your power button indicates your battery charge state: amber for charging, green for charged.

Your device will walk you through your initial setup. Provided you have an Amazon account already, this will take less than 5 minutes to complete. The full procedure is detailed below for those not fully familiar with these devices. If at any time you need to access your settings menus, you can click on the Gear icon on the top of the screen, which will give you access to the various settings on the device.

Firing Up Your Kindle for the First Time

The Kindle Fire comes packaged with a wall charger. Carefully remove the device from the packaging. The Kindle's battery will be partially charged, but it's best to charge it for at least three hours before using the device. To power up the device:

1. Insert the power cable into the base of the device, between the power button and the headphone input.
2. Plug the other end of the adapter into a wall outlet to begin charging the device.
3. An LED on the power button indicates when the device is partially or fully charged. It will glow amber when it is charging and change to green when the device is fully charged.

The Kindle will automatically turn on when you plug it in.

An orange arrow will appear on your device, indicating that it is locked. To unlock the device, slide your finger across the screen to the left, starting on the arrow and dragging it across the screen. This finger motion is sometimes called "swiping."

Turning the Device On/Off

The power button on your Kindle Fire serves several functions.

4. To turn your device on or off, press and hold the button until a confirmation window pops up on the screen.
5. To put the device in sleep mode, press and release the button quickly.

6. To reboot the device, press and hold the power button for 20 seconds. The device will turn off. Restart your Kindle by pressing the power button again.

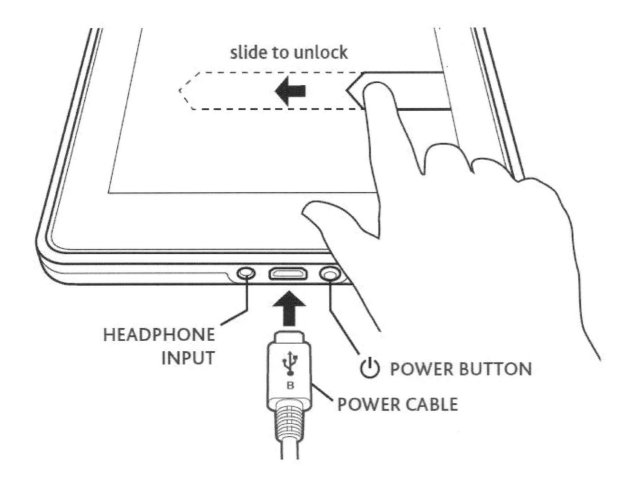

TIP: Like any electronic device, the Kindle Fire will "freeze" from time to time. If this happens, follow the rebooting procedure detailed above. It's normal for this to happen on occasion. If it happens consistently, however, you may want to consider contacting Amazon's customer support staff.

How to navigate the touch-screen

The touch-screen is one of the Kindle Fire's standout features. Using it is literally as easy as pointing your finger.

To use the touch-screen, start by unlocking your device. Pull the orange arrow to the left by placing your finger on the screen—only light pressure is necessary—and pulling as if you were physically pulling the arrow. This "swiping" motion will quickly become second nature.

The basic methods of navigating the Kindle Fire are:

- To select an option, link or menu item on the screen, "press" the appropriate button by tapping it with your finger.
- To advance one page forward, tap the right-hand side of the screen
- To page backward, tap the left-hand side of the screen
- To bring up an alternate menu while using an application or eBook, tap the center of the screen

TIP: Screen protectors are thin plastic coverings that can help protect your Kindle's screen from dirt and scratches. They're inexpensive, and will extend the life of your device. Searching for "Kindle Fire screen protector" at Amazon.com will show listings from several vendors.

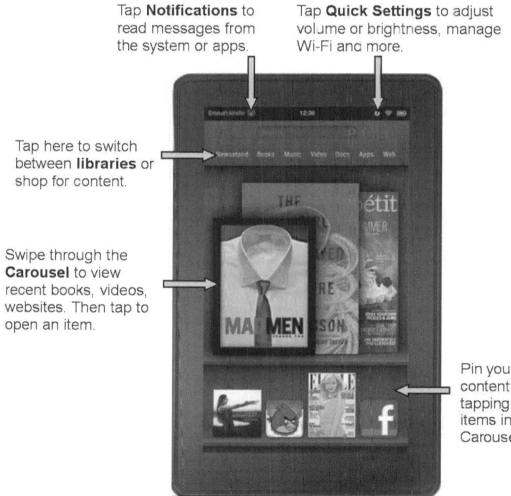

Tap **Notifications** to read messages from the system or apps.

Tap **Quick Settings** to adjust volume or brightness, manage Wi-Fi and more.

Tap here to switch between **libraries** or shop for content.

Swipe through the **Carousel** to view recent books, videos, websites. Then tap to open an item.

Pin your **favorite** content here by tapping and holding items in the Carousel.

Figure 1: The Kindle interface and controls

Registering/Setting Up the Device

When you first plug in and boot up your Kindle, it will automatically guide you through the registration process. You will need an Amazon account to register the device to use all of its features. The automatic process is easy. The first screen will ask for your username and password for your wireless connection. Fill in the fields and let the device connect. Once it does, fill in your email address and password for your Amazon account. The device will register itself and you'll receive an email confirmation at the email address associated with your Amazon account.

If you did not go through the registration process when starting the device, take the following steps to complete registration of the device:

1. Tap the Gear icon at the top of the screen, to the right of the clock and to the left of the battery indicator.
2. Select Wi-Fi
3. Select your wireless network
4. Fill in your password
5. The device will read "connected" to the right of your wireless network name when it is online

Registering the Device
1. Tap the Gear Icon
2. Select "More"
3. Select "My Account"
4. Fill in the appropriate email address and password for your account

On the keyboard, you'll notice a key next to the spacebar with ".com" written on it. Use this to append URLs that have those domains—Gmail.com, etc.—to save yourself extra keystrokes!

Your account information, including any eBooks you've purchased, will be synched to your device automatically.

TIP: You can deregister your device from the "My Account" menu if you want to give it to someone as a gift or if you change your Amazon profile.

Figure 2 The Kindle Settings menu

Battery charging life

Your Kindle Fire battery will be partially charged when you receive the device. Because the total amount of charge varies, you may have to leave it plugged in for a few hours to charge it fully, or charging may take as little as an hour.

If your battery is not charging, check the power adapter's connections to make sure they are fully seated in the device and in the electrical socket.

Your Kindle Fire will provide you with approximately 8 hours of battery life for low-level activities such as reading eBooks. If you're surfing the web or downloading files, the battery will drain faster. Here are a few techniques for conserving battery power and prolonging its life:

- Turn off Wi-Fi when you're not actively downloading files or browsing the Internet.
- If you're listening to audio or watching a video, use the headphones. Using the Kindle's speakers requires much more power.
- Reduce your screen's brightness.
- Once every 30 days, allow your battery to drain completely and then recharge it to full.

TIP: Your Kindle Fire uses a lithium ion battery. Battery performance can degrade at extreme temperatures. Batteries discharge faster in cold temperatures, so warm up your device before turning it on in cold environments. Avoid leaving your Kindle in a car in the summertime or other extremely hot environments; which can cause permanent battery damage.

Navigating the Carousel interface

The carousel interface on the Kindle Fire home-screen allows you to quickly browse recently used content. Items are added to the carousel in chronological order. For example, if you read a newspaper in the morning and a book in the afternoon, the newspaper will appear at the front of the carousel, with the newspaper right behind it.

Navigate the carousel by swiping your finger in either direction—left to right, or right to left. The items revolve as if they were on a merry-go-round. To open any item, tap on it.

TIP: You can "fling" the carousel around very quickly by moving your finger more quickly across the screen. Moving your finger more slowly will advance the items at a lower speed.

If you change the orientation of your device from a portrait to landscape view, the content will automatically shift to accommodate the orientation. Try it.

TIP: Wondering what the difference is between "portrait mode" and "landscape mode?" It's simply the angle at which you're holding your Kindle. Portrait mode is the same way you'd hold a piece of paper to read it—the page is vertically longer than it is wide. With portrait mode, you tilt the Kindle to the side, making it wider than it is tall. As you switch back and forth between modes, your Kindle will automatically rearrange its display so that text and pictures appear right-side-up.

Finding Kindle libraries (Books, Videos, etc.)

The home-screen on your Kindle Fire is the starting point for just about everything you'll do with the device. The home-screen includes your carousel, links to popular destinations such as Facebook, Amazon and IMDb (Internet Movie Database), and allows you to search for content. Along the top of the screen, just below the search bar, you'll find a menu with links to Newsstand, Books, Music, Video, Docs, Apps, and Web.

Figure 3 The Carousel Showing an App and Several Books

Newsstand   Books   Music   Video   Docs   Apps   Web

Figure 4: The Menu at the top of your home-screen.

Tap on any menu item to go to the corresponding section. When you open your libraries of books, videos, music and so forth, you can switch between using a list view and a grid view. The grid view presents you with thumbnail images of the covers of your books and magazines, while the list view shows smaller thumbnails but more written detail.

Newsstand: The Newsstand section of your Kindle Fire contains magazine and newspaper subscriptions. If you don't have any subscriptions yet, you can select the "Store" button on the top of the Newsstand interface to visit the Amazon store. Once you purchase a magazine, it will automatically download to your Kindle. Items more than seven issues old are automatically deleted from your device in order to conserve storage space, but exceptions are possible. For example, if you'd like a magazine to remain on your device after the default storage period, tap and hold the magazine's cover in your library. From the menu that pops up, select "Keep". This will ensure that it is not automatically erased from your device.

After you've accumulated back issues of more than one publication, issues will be sorted by title, enabling you to easily browse your library of that particular publication.

Figure 5: The Newsstand

Newspapers are also accessed from the Newsstand menu. You can subscribe to new newspapers by selecting the "Store" button, just as you did for the magazines.

Magazines and newspapers can be displayed in two different ways. Tap the middle of the screen when you're reading a magazine or newspaper and an "options" menu will appear. You can choose between "Text" and "Page" view by clicking on the icon at the top right of the screen. Text view provides only the text of an article, while Page view shows you the magazine's original layout, including illustrations, just as it appeared on paper. You can adjust the size of the text by clicking the **Aa** icon.

TIP: Some magazines and newspapers don't come in the regular Newsstand format, but are instead provided as apps. If you want to purchase one of these, you have to buy the subscription in the Apps store and download the app to read the periodical.

Books library. The Books section of your library contains all of the eBooks you've purchased from Amazon. Once you register your device, the titles and thumbnails are downloaded. The entire text of the book isn't downloaded to your Kindle until you actually open the document. To open a book, simply tap on its cover thumbnail or—if you're viewing in list view—tap on the text next to the title.

Briefly: Free as a bird

You'll find many classic books available free for the Kindle because they're in the "Public Domain," meaning the books are no longer under copyright restrictions. They include many of the classics, from Jane Austin to Edgar Allen Poe. In addition to Public Domain titles, many current popular books are available free in Kindle format during certain promotional periods. More on that later.

Figure 6: The Books Menu. Most of the books pictured here are in the Public Domain and available free from Amazon.

Like magazines, you can navigate your book library by tapping the right-hand side of the screen, which moves you forward. Tapping the left-hand side of the screen moves you back a page. You can tap the center of your screen to bring up the contextual menu at the bottom of the screen. This allows you to adjust the font size, to go to a specific section or page of a book, to add a comment, or to search the book for particular text.

TIP: If you're using reference books, it's much easier to simply search for text you're trying to locate instead of manually paging through the book or scanning its Table of Contents.

Music library. If you've ever wanted a music player that does much more than simply play music, you're in luck. The Kindle Fire allows you to download your own music to the device or buy songs or albums directly from Amazon. When you first access your Kindle's Music section, you'll see the following screen:

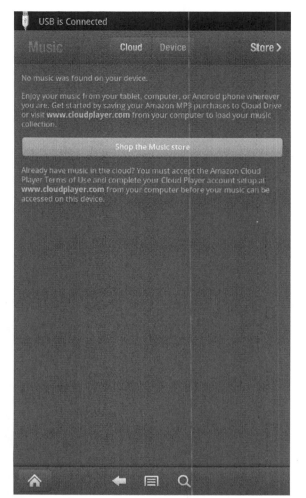

Figure 7: The Kindle Fire music section (before any files are added).

Notice the "**Store>**" link in the upper right-hand section of the screen. Tapping the Store button allows you to shop for music to add to your library. Notice the "Cloud" and "Device" buttons at the top of the screen. Those buttons allow you to play music that you might have stored directly on your device, as well as additional music you may have stored in the Amazon Cloud. The large call-to-action button labeled "Shop the Music Store" enables just that—it's another link to Amazon's music store.

Storing some of your music files in the Cloud can help you conserve space on your device. Either way, you can listen to all of it (although listening to music stored in the Cloud requires a Wi-Fi connection). You can manage the storage of your music by visiting CloudPlayer.com and signing in with your Amazon credentials.

Everyone with an Amazon account has access to 5 Gigabytes of free storage space, with more space available for an annual fee.

We will discuss how to copy music—and all kinds of other files—to your Kindle Fire in the section of this book called **Using a Mini USB Connection to Transfer Content.**

Touch the "Shop the Music Store" button and you'll see the following screen, which will be slightly different for you, depending upon what types of music you've purchased from Amazon previously.

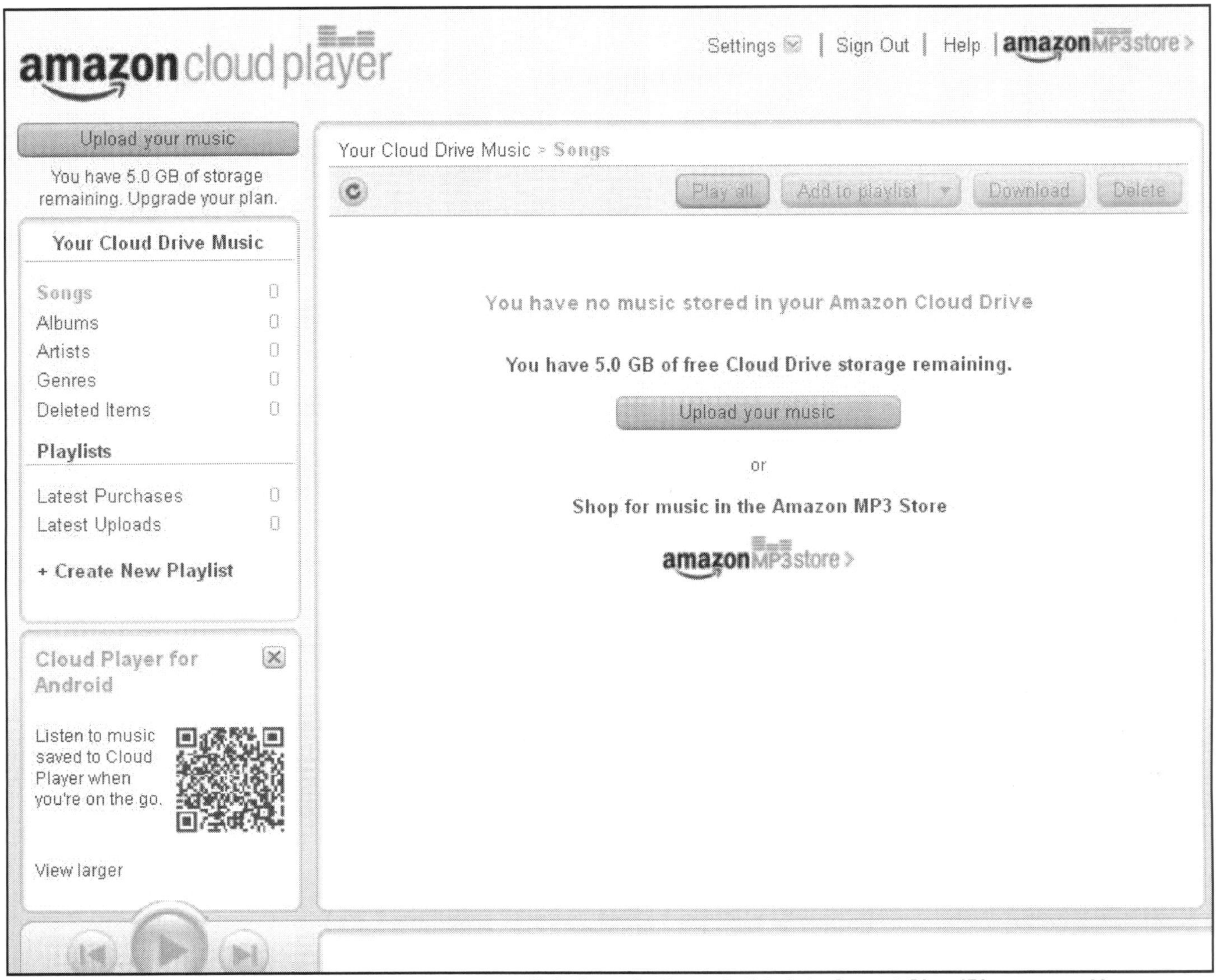

Figure 7a. Amazon allows you to securely store digital music through this interface at CloudPlayer.com. You can play your tunes on your Kindle, PC, Mac, iPad or any Android device. The Amazon Cloud Drive enables you to place all your music in one location and make it accessible everywhere you have an Internet connection.

Briefly: What the heck is 'Whispernet' and 'Whispersync?'

If you've just joined the Kindle party and never bought an early black-and-white E-ink Kindle, you might be curious about the term "Whispernet" mentioned on Amazon eBook listings. Whispernet was a cellular network Amazon cobbled together to deliver eBooks to early Kindle users. It was designed to be as economical as possible yet not burden Kindle users with a monthly service fee. In those days, Wi-Fi wasn't as ubiquitous as today, so Whispernet was needed to deliver content to Kindle users away from home.

Today with the Kindle Fire, there isn't much need for Whispernet. Wi-Fi is a good solution for broadband content delivery while enabling Amazon to keep the Fire's price-tag low as possible.

The other term, "Whisper**sync**," allows you to seamlessly access content using more than one device. For example, imagine you fell asleep last night reading a book on your Kindle Fire. And now, it's the following morning, and you're riding the bus to work—but you left your Kindle Fire at home. So, you pull out your iPhone and launch its Kindle app. The book automatically opens at the point you stopped reading the previous night. Whispersync also remembers all your bookmarks and how far along you've watched each of your videos.

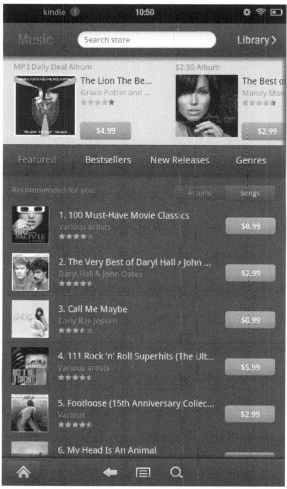

Figure 8: The Shop the Music Store interface

Note the circle with the "1" in it on the top of the screen. The "1" indicates that the Kindle Fire has 1 message for you. In this case, clicking on it will remind me that I can transfer files to my device with my USB connection.

Video library. The Video section of the Kindle Fire is, for many users, the most exciting of all. Your Kindle Fire purchase comes with a free one-month trial of Amazon Prime, giving you access to a huge library of movies that you can watch for free. You can also choose to pay for movies or television shows that aren't part of the Amazon Prime deal. There are literally thousands of movies that you can choose from on this service.

Scrolling through movies is easy. A picture of the interface is shown below. Use your finger to "See More" of any category or simply browse through the movies by "pulling" them, as you would with the carousel on your home-screen.

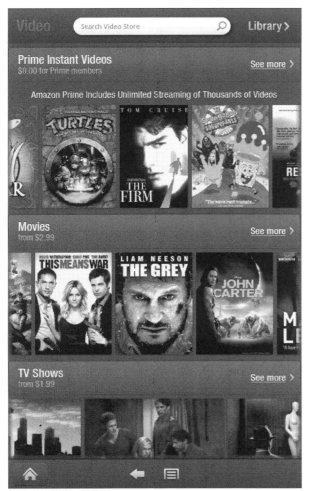

Figure 9: The Video Screen. Prime (free) movies are on top.

Documents Library. Your Kindle Fire can handle a variety of electronic documents, including these formats:

- BMP
- GIF
- HTML
- JPEG
- Microsoft Word (DOC and DOCX)
- MOBI
- PDF
- PNG
- PRC
- RTF
- TXT

Apps are available to expand the functionality of your Kindle Fire for productivity, which we'll discuss further. Even without any additional office apps, your Kindle can open any of the above-named formats and you can handle PDFs in their native format. If you're a student, you can read PDF documents related to your classes right on your Kindle.

You can load documents onto your Kindle using a Mini-USB cable connected to your computer. An even easier method of transferring documents is via email. Your Kindle has a Send-to-Kindle email address associated with it. It will usually be YourName@Kindle.com. If you're unsure of your Kindle's email address, view "Manage Your Kindle" page at Amazon's site, Amazon.com/myk. In the left sidebar, click the link "Manage Your Devices" and you'll see a list of Kindles associated with your account, along with their Send-to-Kindle email addresses. You can send documents to this address and they will automatically be added to your Docs library. This is a handy feature in instances when you find interesting documents online, and want to preserve them for later reference.

Any documents you send to your Kindle via email or USB are stored directly on the device, not in Amazon's Cloud.

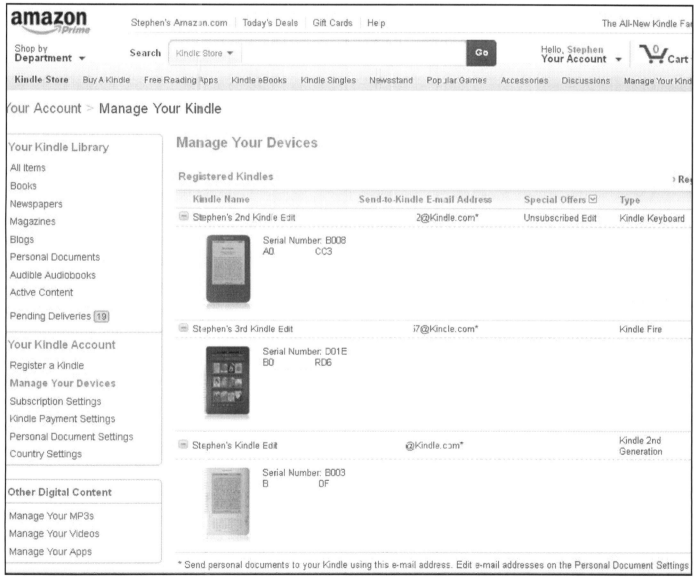

Figure 9a. The 'Manage Your Kindle' page at Amazon.com/myk. Here you can perform many administrative tasks and access all your digital media.

Briefly: Urgent business opportunities in Nigeria

Like just about everyone else, I have friends who like to forward emails with content they consider humorous or interesting. Of course, this is highly dependent on personal tastes. If you don't want your Kindle cluttered with funny cat pictures and urban legends, avoid sharing your Send-to-Kindle email address. It's the same thing as giving someone permission to save a file directly on your device.

Apps Library. Apps is likely to be one of the most popular selections on your home-screen menu. The Apps section allows you to purchase and download Apps for your Kindle Fire, which greatly expands its functionality. Just as with the other sections of your Kindle Fire home-screen, there is a **Store >** button that enables you to shop via Amazon. You'll also be able to download one paid application for free on a daily basis, which is one of the perks of being an Amazon Prime member with a Kindle.

Amazon's Android App Store is divided into categories: Entertainment, Lifestyle, New, and so forth. Take a look through the Apps available and you'll find an incredible range of products that allow you to use your Kindle in novel ways. Everything from games to office suites is available.

The initial screen you'll get when you select the Apps button on your menu is your Library:

Figure 10: The Kindle Fire App Library

To use any of your Apps, simply click on its icon, and it will launch. Note that the Weather Channel, Pandora, and ESPN Score icons in the illustration above have an arrow superimposed on the icon. This indicates I've purchased those apps but haven't yet downloaded them to my device. Clicking on the "Device" icon near the top of the screen will take you to a Library shelf that only shows those Apps that are actually loaded onto your device.

TIP: Even though many apps are free, you still need to have "One-Click Payment" enabled at Amazon in order to "purchase" them. Ensure you have a default credit card established with your Amazon account so that you can take advantage of the many free offerings.

Web. The Kindle Fire's extensive web-browsing capability is what differentiates it from most tablets. It's powered by Kindle Fire's "Silk" browser, which combines the power of your device and Amazon's Cloud to enable fast, streamlined web browsing.

At the top of the Silk browser, you'll see these buttons and functions:

Figure 11: Buttons from left to right: Home, Back, Forward, Menu, Bookmark, Full Screen

Clicking on the "Menu" option gives you access to another range of functions, including Add Bookmark, Share Page, Find in Page, History, Downloads, and Settings.

Clearing Your Browser History

Online privacy—and security, for that matter—sometimes depends upon being able to erase the Internet history of your browser. It's a simple procedure on your Kindle Fire:

1. Open your web browser
2. Select the menu button
3. Select "History:
4. Select "Clear All" from the upper right corner

Reading View: Reading View is a browser layout that is optimized for reading. It takes the content you're looking at and converts it to a format that makes it easier on the eyes. On web pages where this function is available, you'll see an icon that looks like a small pair of glasses on your menu bar. Click on it and you'll get to see the page in Reading View. Reading View features bigger, bolder text and eliminates multiple-column layouts that can be nuisances on tablet devices such as the Kindle Fire.

To navigate to a page, simply put your cursor in the URL bar—just touch the URL bar with your finger—and type in the desired URL in the keyboard that pops up on the screen. Hit "Go" to go to the page.

TIP: If you have trouble hitting the keyboard keys accurately, turn the device so that it is in a landscape orientation. This increases the size of the keys and makes it a lot easier to type accurately.

Designating Favorites

The Silk browser makes designating favorites very easy. There is a bookmark icon on the main menu bar for the browser.

Click on the bookmark bar and you'll be taken to a screen where you have the option of adding the current page to your favorites. This is indicated by a "+" mark on an icon of the page that is displayed on the screen, pictured below.

Figure 12: The Kindle Favorites Page. Note the "+" Sign on the First Page, "Buzzfeed.com".

To add the favorite to your list, simply click on the "+" sign and it's done! To access your existing bookmarks at any time, click on the Bookmark icon and you'll be taken to this page.

The Status Bar and Option Bar

The Status Bar is located at the top if your Kindle screen. It shows, from right to left, your name, an indicator that displays how many messages you have—the circle with the "1" in it below—the current time, your **Gear Icon**, your wireless connectivity state and network signal strength and your battery charge status. The **Gear Icon** opens up the **Options Bar**, which gives you control over most of your Kindle Fire's settings. Click on the **Gear Icon**, pictured below.

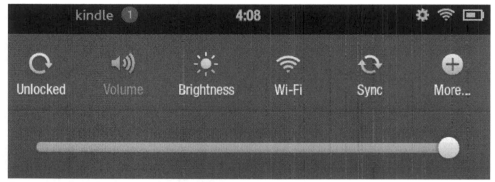

Figure 13: Click on the Gear Icon to Access the Status Bar

Once you click on the Gear Icon, you'll get the following, basic version of your Kindle Fire's Settings:

Figure 14: The Expanded Settings Menu

Using these settings is detailed in the section of Chapter 2 labeled **Guide to Quick Settings**.

Using a Mini-USB Connection to Transfer Content

The Kindle Fire can connect to your PC or Mac with a Mini-USB cable. This is a cable with a standard USB connection on one end and a smaller connection on the other—the smaller connection being identical to the one that you use to charge your device.

If your computer has Windows 2000 or later—or Macintosh OS X 10.2 or later—when you connect the Kindle Fire via USB, the device appears as a "removable disk." To transfer filess from your computer to your Kindle, you simply "drag" them from their folder on the computer onto the Kindle folder.

If you're purchasing something from Amazon and you want to transfer it directly to your Kindle via USB, the procedure is very simple: After completing your purchase, visit the "Manage Your Kindle" page at Amazon.com/myk. Navigate to the "All Items" section and locate the item you want to download to your device.

Once you've found the desired title, follow these steps:

1. Click on the "Actions" button to the right of the title that you want to transfer. Here, I've clicked on "The Castle of Otranto" by Horace Walpole.

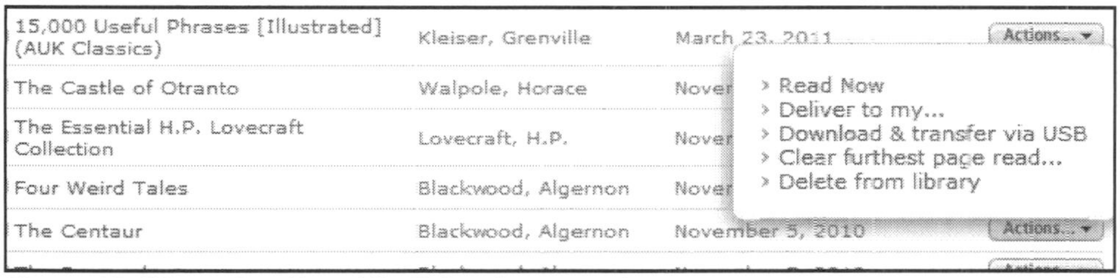

Figure 15. 'Managing Your Kindle' webpage at Amazon.com.

2. A pop-up box appears with five options. Select "Download & transfer via USB." Next, you'll see a page like this on your computer:

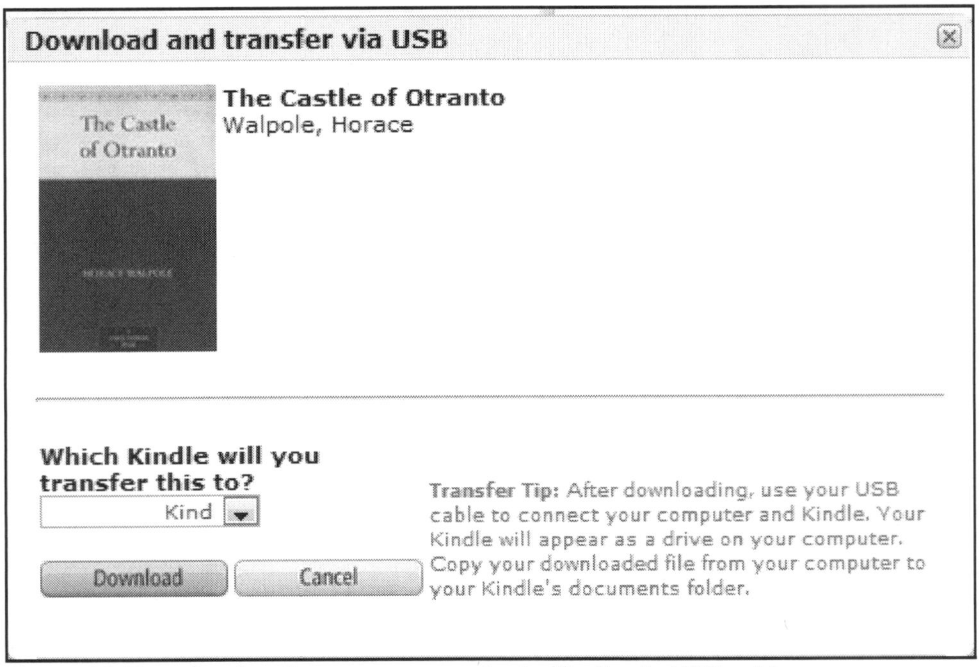

Figure 16. Downloading from your computer to Kindle via USB cable.

The dropdown list will give you a list of your devices, including the Amazon Cloud storage option.

After you've downloaded the content, it will appear in your "My Kindle Content" folder (unless you've set up your preferences differently).

To transfer the file to your Kindle Fire, simply drag and drop it from the My Kindle Content folder to the appropriate folder on your Kindle.

Any content that you transfer to your Kindle Fire via USB will be ordered into the correct shelf on your Library. Books will appear in Books, Music in Music, and so on.

Using this procedure, you can drag and drop any kind of content, as long as the format is supported by the Kindle. If you've been looking for a neat way to back up your music collection—like your old CDs or music you have in iTunes—this is it.

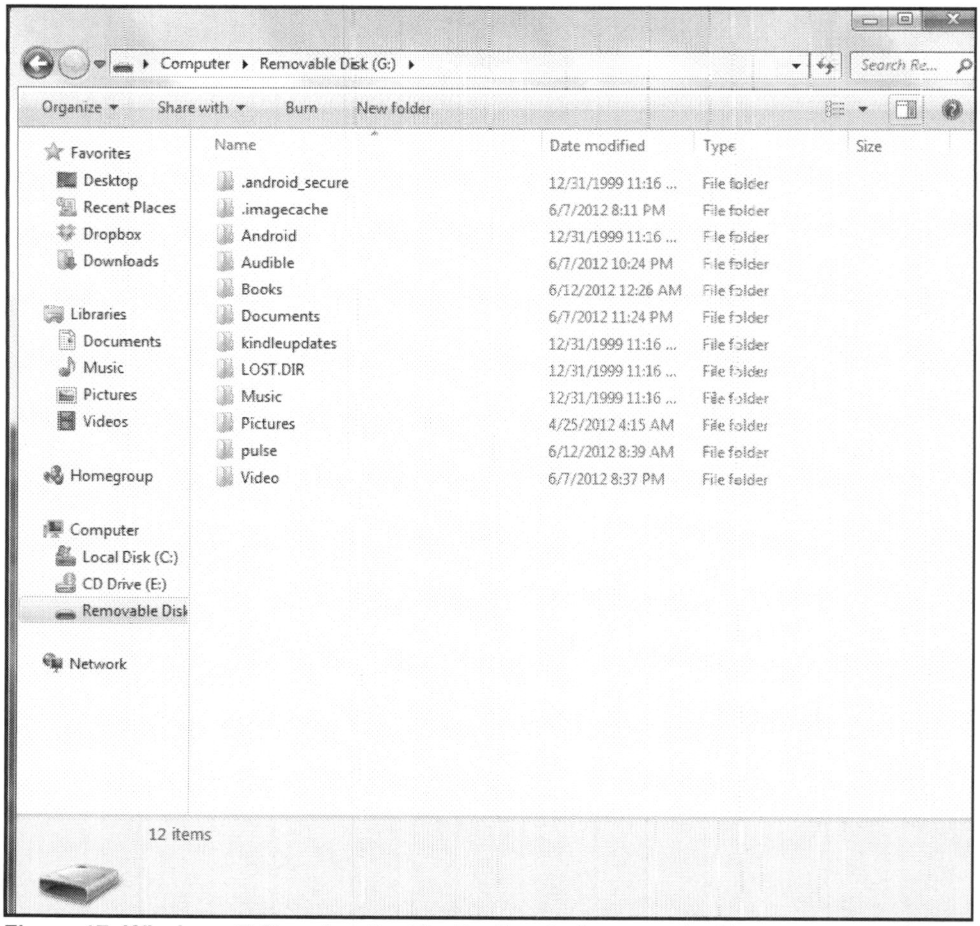

Figure 17: Windows 7 Showing the Kindle directories on a desktop computer. Connected via a Mini-USB cable, the Kindle device appears as a "Removable Disk" on the left.

TIP: Some eBook formats available outside Amazon aren't supported by the Kindle. Luckily, there are free conversion tools available for making virtually any document Kindle-compatible. One such tool is the "Calibre" program, which we'll discuss in detail later.

Kindle Fire HD: New models with improved display and sound

One year after the Kindle Fire's introduction, Amazon added an 8.9-inch screen, a 4G wireless option, and several more refinements, making the Kindle Fire even more compelling.

The original Fire's home screen "bookshelf" metaphor was replaced by a sleeker carousel of icons, which responds more crisply to the touch. Content categories, such as "Apps" and "Books" appear as before, along with additions like "Games" and "Photos." A new photo-viewing app allows you to send pictures to your Amazon CloudDrive account and view them on the Kindle.

As before, favorite content can be "pinned" to the home screen, and now that menu is accessed by tapping a star icon at the bottom of the screen. (To add an item, press and hold the item's icon, then hit "Add to Favorites.")

The new Fires are dubbed "HD" because of the improved screen sharpness. They also have mini-HDMI jacks, which allow you to connect your device to a high-definition TV. The HD's sound quality is vastly improved, thanks to its Dolby audio circuitry and beefier speakers.

A new feature parents will appreciate: individual accounts for children, with parent-approved time limits for certain activities, such as reading, movies, and games.

In addition to the improved video display, a new "reader" app for the Kindle HD improves the reading experience. A new navigation bar allows you to change fonts and colors, visit the Table of Contents, share via social networks, and manage bookmarks. The navigation bar also reveals the new "X-Ray" feature offering handy access to background information about the topic you're reading—for example, you can quickly access the author's biography from Wikipedia. The X-Ray feature can also be accessed while watching videos.

Another new wrinkle, Whispersync for Voice, can synchronize your reading place between audiobooks and the text of the same title, provided you've purchased both formats.

The new Kindle Fires also have a front-facing camera, enabling free Skype video calls. The HD also displays advertisements when the screen is locked, which you can eliminate with a one-time payment of $15.

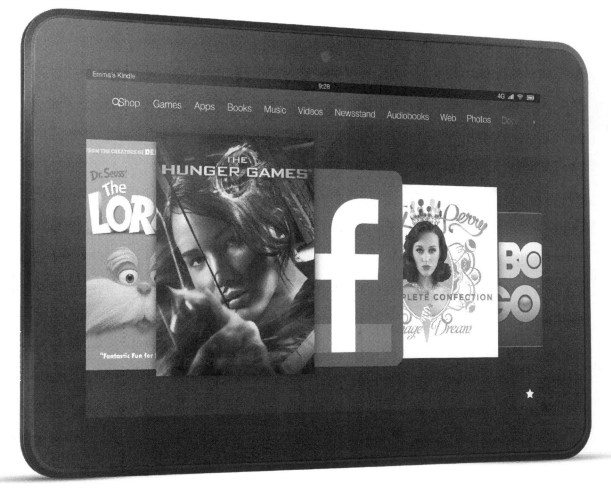

Figure 17A: The Kindle Fire HD with 8.9-inch screen

2 ▶ SETTINGS

We briefly explored the **Status** and **Option Bars** in Chapter 1. Customizing your Kindle Fire will require you to access your **Option Bar**, which is done by clicking on the **Gear Icon** in the **Status Bar**. Details of the various quick settings are given below.

Guide to Quick Settings

Click on the **Gear Icon** in the **Status Bar** to open the following menu.

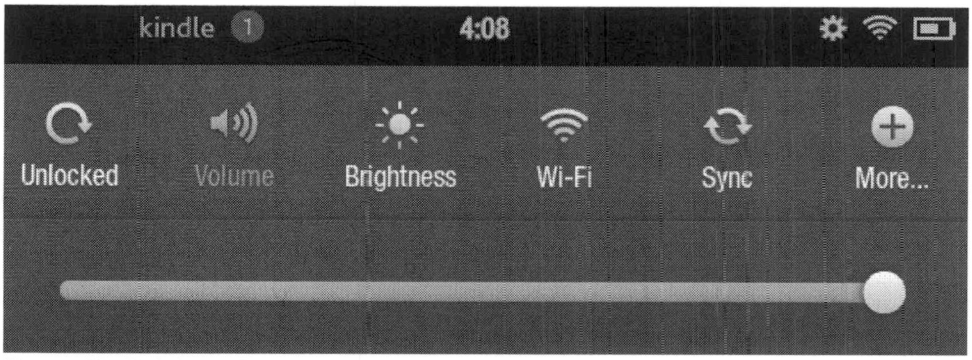

Figure 18. Quick settings.

This menu gives you access to the most common controls that you'll need for your Kindle Fire. **Locking** or **Unlocking** your Kindle Fire refers to the screen rotation feature. To lock it in its current landscape or portrait orientation, press the button. To unlock it so that it changes according to the position in which you're holding it, press the button to toggle it back.

The slider shown in the picture above allows you to adjust settings when they are variable, including the **Volume** and **Brightness** settings

The **Wi-Fi** settings allow you to connect to available wireless networks.

Pressing **Sync** causes your Kindle to check to see if everything on your Kindle Fire is synchronized with your Cloud content. If you've just made a purchase and it hasn't appeared on your Kindle, tap this button to sync with the Cloud.

Press the "**More...**" button and you'll see the following screen, which allows you to adjust more advanced settings:

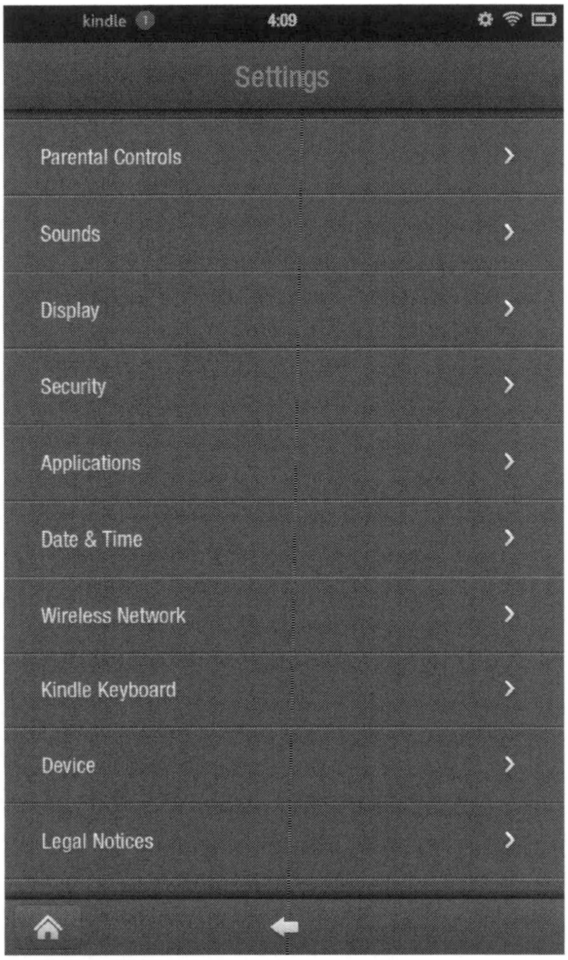

Figure 19: The fully expanded options menu.

The settings offer these options:

Parental Controls allows you to control access to your device. It enables you to create a password that allows you to restrict what your children—or other people using your device—may do with the Kindle Fire. You can block web-surfing, or block the ability to make purchases. If you wish, you can also restrict access to some or all of your content libraries.

The **Sounds** menu allows you to control the sounds that you device emits to alert you of new events—emails, instant messages, etc.—and to control the volume of those notifications.

Your **Display** menu is an important one where battery life is concerned. To maximize your battery life, set the screen to turn off at the soonest practical interval. Also, lower your screen's brightness a bit to conserve more battery juice.

Security is important, and the **Security** menu allows you to require a password to open your Kindle Fire after it times out, or to awaken it from "sleep" mode. If you don't want other users of your Kindle to have access to your emails and other personal messages, password protection is a must.

Applications might have been better named "Apps" to avoid confusion, but that's exactly what this menu allows you to control. Here, you can view all of your different applications and their statuses. You can see which ones are running and which are provided by third parties. To access the settings for any applications, simply touch the appropriate name.

Date & Time controls just that. If you leave the setting on "Automatic" your Kindle will stay accurate.

Wireless Network shows a list of Wi-Fi hotspots in range of your Kindle Fire. You can change the settings for your Wi-Fi setup here or switch to a different network if you wish. Full instructions for connecting to wireless networks are discussed later in this chapter.

Kindle Keyboard allows you to change settings for your keyboard. By default, there is a "quick fix" function enabled for your Kindle. This corrects common typos automatically, similar to some word-processing tools. For some users, however, the quick-fix is a nuisance, particularly if you have friends with names that are close to common English words—you'll type in the name, and it's "corrected" to something else entirely. If you pepper your emails with jargon and abbreviations, the auto-fix feature can be especially annoying. Fortunately, you can turn off the auto-correct feature here. Also, you can prevent your Kindle from automatically capitalizing the first letter after a period, or emitting sounds when you strike a character on your keyboard.

Device is the information center for your Kindle. Here, you'll see information such as how much space you have remaining for storage, what operating system you're using, what your device's serial number is, your Wi-Fi address, and options for installing install software obtained outside Amazon's App Store. You'll also be able to reset your Kindle back to its factory settings, which can be handy if you decide to sell your Kindle or give it to someone else.

Legal Notices gives you information on the licensing status about your Apps and the device itself.

Terms of Service is that long document regarding how you're permitted to use your device that no one ever reads. It's worth it to look it over, however.

Don't be afraid to experiment with these settings. The Kindle Fire, for all of its capabilities, is a simple device in many regards and most of these selections are of the On/Off variety, meaning that there is little to worry about in terms of what you might accidentally do by selecting the incorrect setting.

Viewing Your Amazon Account on the Kindle

When you expand the **Options Bar**, you'll notice that one of the available menu selections is **My Account**. Click on this selection and you'll see the current account to which the Kindle Fire is associated. If you want to switch accounts, simply click the "**Deregister**" button located below the account information. Then your Kindle Fire will be available for registration by someone else.

Using your Kindle Fire is a lot more convenient if you designate a One-Click payment method for your Amazon account. This is easy to do from your desktop computer or from the Kindle's web browser. Here's the procedure:

1. Log into Amazon
2. From the dropdown menu on the top of the page labeled "Hello, [Your Name] ,Your Account" select "Manage Your Kindle"
3. On the left-hand side of the Manage Your Kindle page select "Kindle Payment Settings"

4. You will either have the option to create a One-Click payment method on the next screen or an option to edit your existing method.

How to Control Sounds

Controlling the sounds on your Kindle Fire is easy. Click on "**Sounds**" on the expanded **Options** menu. You'll see this screen:

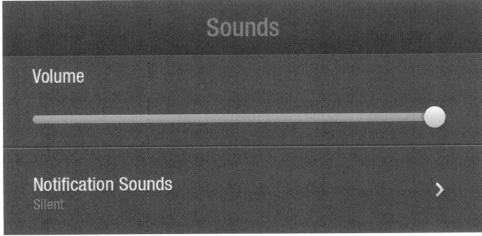

Figure 20: The Sounds menu as you'll first encounter it.

The **Volume** slider is operated by swiping your finger. This will control the output volume on your Kindle Fire. If you connect external speakers to your Kindle, they will probably have their own volume controls as well.

TIP: If you've connected external speakers to your Kindle Fire and the sound is distorted, it's possible that you've overloaded the external speakers. To correct this, reduce the Kindle's volume and increase the volume setting on the external speakers.

Notice that **Notification Sounds** in the above picture is set to "**Silent**". This is the default setting. It's also the best setting if you're trying to conserve battery power. If you want your Kindle Fire to notify you of new events—such as getting an email, receiving an instant message and so forth—you can touch this menu. The following screen will appear:

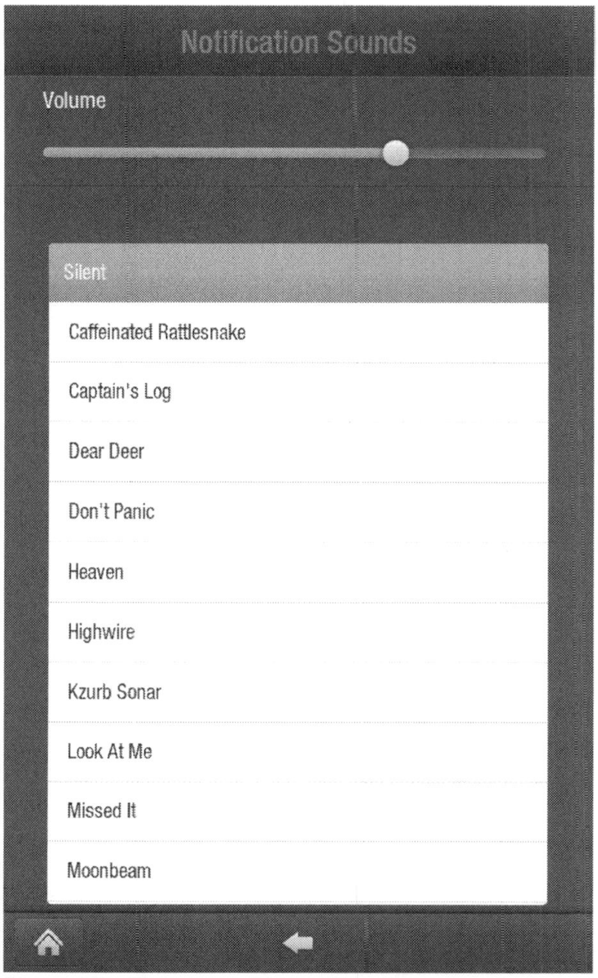

Figure 21: The expanded notification sounds menu. If you use an Android phone, this screen will look familiar. Select any of the available notification tones to set it as your default alert sound. You can use the slider to adjust the volume of your notifications once you do so.

Adjusting Fonts and Other Appearance-Related Items

The Kindle Fire may have a lot of capabilities, but its roots are firmly planted in the world of eReaders. EReaders aren't much fun unless you can adjust the fonts and other display features to make it easy on your eyes. The Kindle Fire's font settings are very similar to what you may be accustomed to with a laptop computer or Android phone. Here are the basics of adjusting your fonts and other display items:

Brightness: The overall brightness of your screen is adjusted from the **Options Bar**. A simple slider allows you to control how bright the display is. This is accessible from the simplified bar that comes up when you first click on the **Gear Icon**. This makes it easy to quickly adjust the settings to accommodate different lighting conditions indoors or out.

Fonts, Typeface and Other EBook Settings: Adjusting the typeface and fonts, as well as related settings, in eBooks is very easy on the Kindle Fire. Open up an eBook and tap on the center of the screen quickly. The following menu will slide up from the bottom:

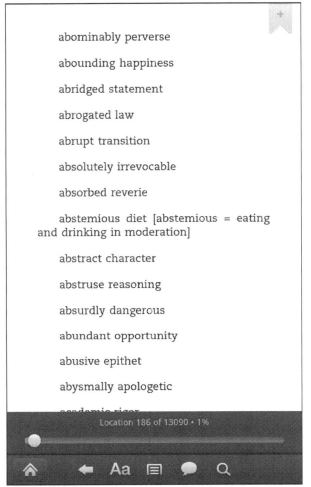

Figure 22: The Simplified eBook menu. Note the '+' on the Bookmark icon on the top. This allows you to add a Bookmark on the current page.

To access the advanced font settings for your display, click on the "**Aa**" icon on the bottom of the screen. This will open up the menu shown here:

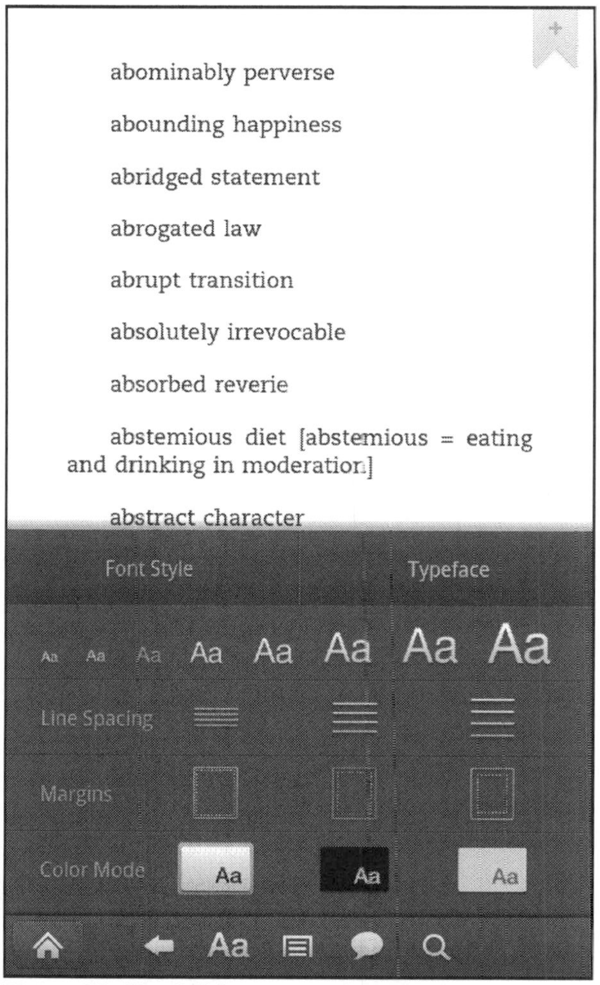

Figure 23: The full font menu for eBooks.

This menu contains several settings that you can use to customize the look and feel of the books you're reading.

Aa changes the size of the font to make text larger or smaller. Simply click on a selection until you find the best font for you.

Line Spacing means just what it says. You'll find that this feature is particularly useful because some eBooks have tight line spacing. Adding a bit more line spacing can make reading more comfortable.

Margins controls the amount of blank space between the edges of the screen and the text.

Color Mode allows you to choose between black text on a white screen, white text on a black screen, or black text on a sepia-colored screen.

Click on "**Typeface**" to see the following menu.

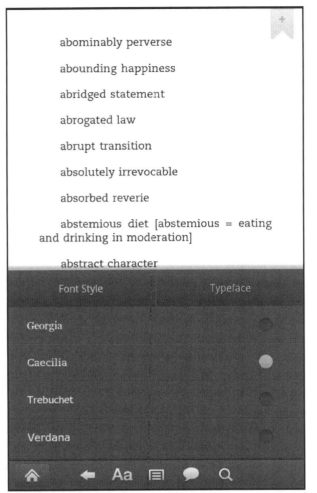

Figure 24: The Typeface Menu expanded.

There are more selections than can fit in the illustration above. You can scroll down by dragging the list up with your finger. The typefaces available include:

- Arial
- Caecilia
- Courier
- Georgia
- Lucida
- Times New Roman
- Trebuchet
- Verdana

Using these controls, you can set up the display of any eBook so that it is as comfortable as possible for your eyes.

TIP: Although it's possible to read eBooks on a Kindle Fire in a darkened room, doing so can induce eyestrain. You'll find it's a bit more comfortable if there's at least some ambient light available. Also, some experts advocate the "20/20/20" rule for eReaders. When you're reading a screen held closely to your face, take a break every 20 minutes and gaze at an object about 20 feet away for about 20 seconds to give your eyes a rest.

Setting up Wi-Fi

The Kindle Fire can connect to just about any wireless network. Before you get started, however, you'll want to learn a little bit about wireless security. Your Kindle Fire is a relatively save device, but it's good to be careful.

Public Wi-Fi

Publicly available Wi-Fi networks are convenient, but they can be risky. To avoid having any of your personal information intercepted when you're accessing secure webpages—like activities on Facebook or banking sites—wait until you're on your home network.

Connecting with Wi-Fi

To connect your Kindle to your Wi-Fi network, follow these steps:

1. Select the **Gear Icon** on the **Status Bar**
2. Select "**More...**" from the menu
3. Select "**Wireless Network**" from the expanded menu
4. The following screen will appear

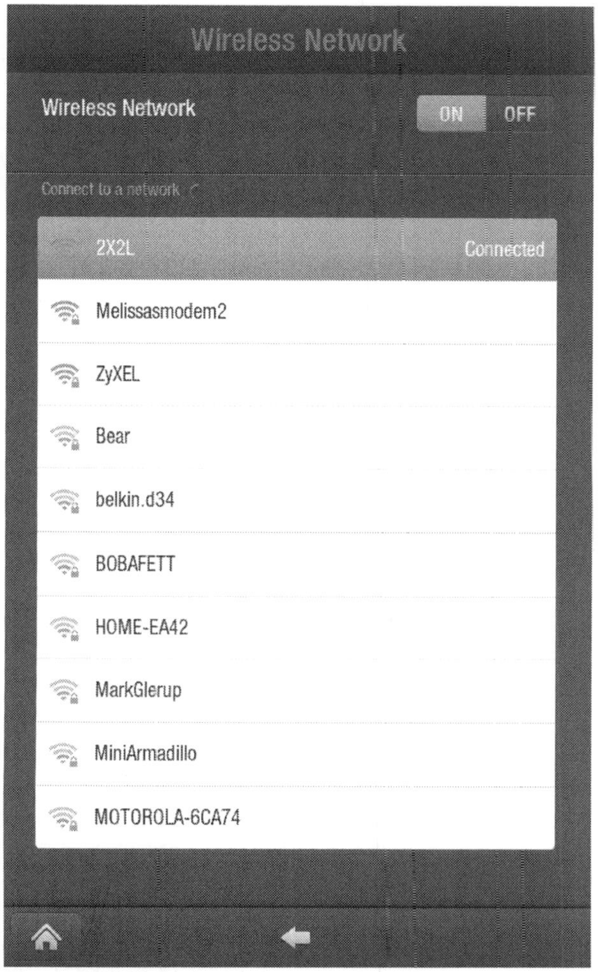

Figure 25: The wireless network screen

Verify that the **Wireless Network** is set to "**On**".

Below the **Wireless Network On/Off** toggle, you'll see a list of available networks. Networks listed with a padlock icon require a password. If you're at an establishment that offers free Wi-Fi, the padlock probably won't appear. The current network to which you are connected will be highlighted in orange. In this case, my Kindle Fire is connected to the 2X2L network.

To connect to a different network, simply click on the name. The following screen will appear.

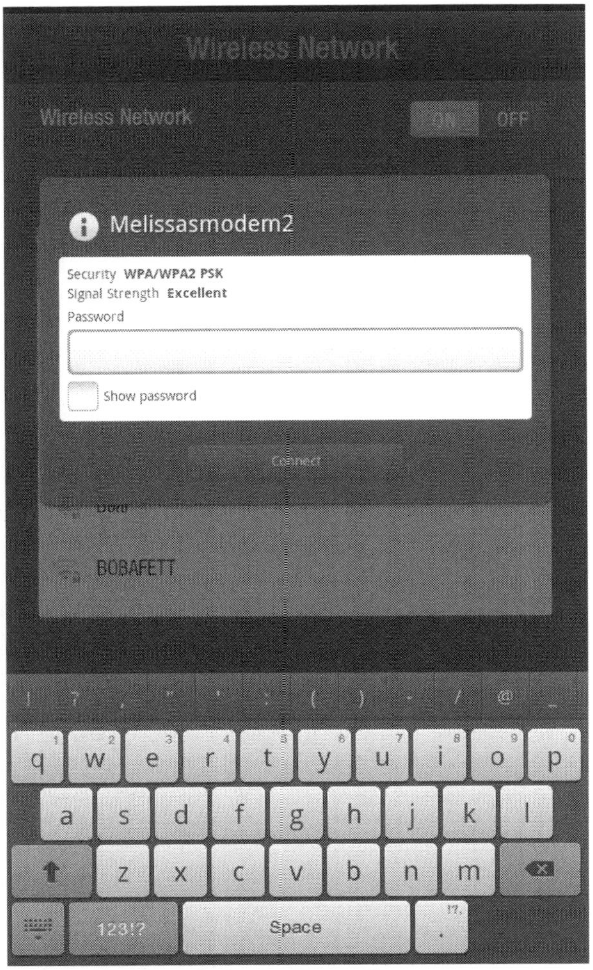

Figure 26: The wireless connection screen

Fill in the appropriate password, hit connect, and your Kindle Fire will connect to the network.

TIP: Many wireless network passwords are very long and are completely random, making it difficult to enter the password without making a mistake. Select "Show Password" so that you can see what you're typing and verify that you're typing the password correctly.

Using the Keyboard

If you have a smartphone or other touch-screen device, you're probably already familiar with the basics of a touch-screen keyboard. If you're not, the learning curve shouldn't be too steep, but there may be some frustration initially. Here are some basic tips to keep in mind.

- It's much easier to type accurately if your Kindle is in landscape mode—the keyboard is enlarged, giving you more room to type.
- Use your thumbs to type while holding the Kindle Fire in your hand
- Your keyboard will autocorrect words for you, but you can turn this feature off, which may actually be more desirable. See the previous section, **Guide to Quick Settings** for details.
- A screen protector can prevent fingerprint smudges from building up on your screen resulting from typing.
- Several different keyboards can be accessed by tapping the **SHIFT** key, the **123!?** key and the **.+= key.** Sound complicated? It's really not—after you've gotten some practice it'll go faster. Let's explore the basics:

Accessing the Keyboard

To open the keyboard, simply tap the screen to place your cursor in any region where you can type. This applies to the browser address bar, libraries, and all other features on the Kindle.

Keyboard Layouts

The basic keyboard layout is shown in below illustration. Note the cursor in the search field. This was the trigger that pulled up the keyboard in this particular instance.

Figure 27: The default keyboard layout.

Notice that there is also a row of common symbols at the top of the keyboard. You can use these instead of pressing the **123!?** button (in most cases). Now, let's take a look at some alternate keyboard layouts.

Tap your **SHIFT** key, which is the upward-pointing arrow at the left of the keyboard. You'll see the keys change to uppercase, as pictured below:

Figure 28: The keyboard in upper case mode.

TIP: The **SHIFT** key turns white when you have the keyboard in uppercase mode. Selecting the white **SHIFT** key turns on the CAPS LOCK feature while the **SHIFT** turns orange. If you don't turn on CAPS LOCK, the keyboard will automatically revert to lower-case mode after you press a key.

Even though a list of common symbols is listed across the top of the keyboard, you sometimes need more. To access more symbols, numerals and more punctuation marks, tap the **123!?** key. The keyboard layout will change to the mode illustrated below:

Figure 29: The 123!? keyboard layout.

To switch back to the default keyboard, tap the **ABC** key.

These three keyboards provide most of what you'll need to handle just about anything you ever have to type. There are occasions, however, when you'll want even more options than these three keyboard layouts afford, and that is where the **.+-** key comes into play. Tap it, and you'll see the keyboard layout pictured below.

Figure 30: The symbol keyboard layout.

The symbol keyboard has some very useful functions:

Search: Allows you to search from any search field without using the button on the actual search page.
Go: Takes you to an address that you specify in a URL bar
.com: Fills in the most common top level domain for you so you don't have to

These keys will show up when appropriate.

To dismiss the keyboard, press the key at the left of the bottom row, the one with the keyboard icon and the downward-pointing arrow.

3 ▶ SHOP FOR CONTENT ON THE KINDLE

Your Kindle Fire is a capable tablet computer, a handy productivity tool, and much more—but on top of all that, it's a lean, mean shopping machine. It's optimized for shopping at Amazon, of course, giving you instant access to the vast range of products available there. The Kindle Fire—and other Kindle models, for that matter—allows you to instantly network with the Amazon store, whether you're using the web browser or directly through the digital media stores.

Searching for Content on the Newsstand

We've briefly mentioned the Newsstand already, but here's a quick refresher:

1. From any screen, select the "**Home**" button
2. Select "**Newsstand**" from the top menu bar, right below the search bar.
3. The content you own will be listed on the next screen
4. Select "**Store >**" to visit the Amazon store

The next screen displays images of magazines and links to Newspapers and the Kindle Bookstore. Clicking on the menu items "**Browse Magazines**", "**Browse Newspapers**" or "**Browse Kindle Bookstore**" will bring up a category menu. Use the menu to browse available content.

To search, simply enter your desired term in the **Search** field at the upper center of your screen. I searched for "Science Fiction," for example, and the following selection of Sci-Fi magazines appeared in the search results. The list extends beyond the bottom of the screen. You can scroll through your results by sliding the list up and down with your finger.

Figure 31: A Newsstand search for 'Science Fiction.'

TIP: The search feature is intuitive. If you can't remember the full name of a magazine but type in a partial title, your Kindle will usually manage to complete the title for you. For example, typing "cosmo" will show Cosmopolitan Magazine among the results. Typing in "home" will show magazines with "home" in the title.

Click on any given magazine and you'll get more info about it. Below, I clicked on Asimov's Science Fiction Magazine and got the following summary of the offering.

TIP: If you're not sure whether or not you want to subscribe to a particular magazine, there is an option to buy just the current issue. In nearly every regard, the Kindle's Newsstand functions like a real-life newsstand.

Figure 32: Asimov's Summary from Newsstand.

TIP: It's possible to subscribe to magazines from sources other than the Amazon Newsstand. So don't be discouraged if you can't find your favorite titles through Amazon; they may be available elsewhere in a Kindle-friendly format. Also, in Chapter 10, **Feed Your Kindle with Web Content**, we'll explore ways to download leading newspapers and magazines to your Kindle, completely free of charge.

You can buy newspapers through the Newsstand using this same procedure. Be sure to note the subscription price. Magazine and newspaper subscribers are billed on a monthly basis. Unlike the usual procedure with print editions—where you might be asked to pay for an entire year of issues up-front—you may cancel a subscription through the Kindle newsstand at any time.

Most magazines on the Kindle Newsstand come with a "free trial" offer, which usually equates to one free issue. Just remember to cancel your subscription if you don't want to be billed for subsequent issues. You can manage your subscriptions through the "Manage Your Kindle" page on Amazon's website, Amazon.com/myk.

You can browse newspapers by region or you can search for specific titles. If you're looking for papers in New York, you can just type "New York" in the search bar and you'll get a list of newspapers published there.

As mentioned previously, you must have a One-Click payment method enabled at Amazon in order to purchase digital media through the Newsstand.

Browsing and buying books

Amazon is perhaps most famous for its vast selection of books, and the Kindle Fire places its entire library of eBooks at your fingertips. You can purchase Kindle editions directly through the device, or you might prefer shopping at the website using a desktop computer. Here's the procedure for book shopping on the Kindle Fire:

1. Go to your home-screen.
2. Select "**Books**" from the top menu.
3. You'll arrive at your **Library**. Select "**Store >**" at the top left of the screen
4. Welcome to the book store!

Purchasing books is very similar to buying magazines through the Newsstand. You can search for a book using the search field at the top of the screen—or you can browse categories on the right of the screen.

Figure 33: The book store screen

In **Figure 33**, you'll notice there are recommendations at the top of the screen, a Top 100 list below that, and more suggestions below the Top 100. The links on the left allow you to browse books by category.

When you select a title, you'll get a description of the book:

Figure 34: A book description. Try a sample!

Because your Kindle Fire is a full-color device, it's a great tool for viewing comic books and graphic novels.

TIP: If you have more than one Kindle, you can send any content you purchase to each device through the "Manage Your Kindle" page at Amazon.com/myk.

Kindle Buffet: Free books, all you can eat!

One of the best things about Amazon's digital bookstore is that many of its most popular books are offered completely free of charge during brief promotional periods. If you manage to find and download a book while it's offered free, it's yours to keep—forever. It's a great way to sample a new genre, or perhaps discover an author you hadn't noticed before.

kindlebuffet

Home   Free Fiction Bestsellers   Free Nonfiction Bestsellers   Kindle accessories (paid)   Prime Instant V

Editor's Picks: Another baker's dozen of fresh Kindle freebies

Posted on September 19, 2012 by Steve Weber

Dance of the Winnebagos (Jackrabbit Junction Mystery Series #1)

- $3.99 List Price
- See Kindle Price at Amazon.com

Product Description Free Fall Free ParTay! For Two Days Only, Sep. 19th - 20th, "Dance of the Winnebagos" will be FREE! If you like "Dance of the Winnebagos" you might also like these other FREE books:"The Rush," The MoonRush prequel short story. By Carolyn McCray."Liquid Lies," One dead body and two girls with a secret. By Lois Lavrisa."Resistance," One man must infiltrate the hive mind, but will it cost his soul? Travel into the far future! By David Weisman.... Read more

---

amazon.com

Customer Reviews
Average Customer Review
★★★★☆ (79 customer reviews)

79 Reviews

5 star:		(55)
4 star:		(10)
3 star:		(4)
2 star:		(5)
1 star:		(5)

Drummer Boy: A Supernatural Thriller (Sheriff Littlefield Series)

- $2.99 List Price
- See Kindle Price at Amazon.com

Product Description One misfit kid is all that stands between an Appalachian Mountain town and a chilling supernatural force.DRUMMER BOY: A Supernatural ThrillerOn an Appalachian Mountain ridge, young Vernon Ray Davis hears the rattling of a snare drum deep inside a cave

Figure 34a. The home page of KindleBuffet.com. Visit the site for daily Editor's Picks of great Kindle books that have gone free that same day.

I love downloading free books to my Kindles so much, I started a website and newsletter called KindleBuffet.com to help keep track of the very best books currently available free. (The free promotions usually last only a few days, but there's a new crop every day). Take a look, and I'm sure you'll be amazed at the wealth of great books—usually there are several hundred freebies in virtually every category of fiction and nonfiction, every day of the year. And these aren't just the dogs that nobody wants, the selection includes bona-fide bestsellers from the most famous authors in the world. You may never have to pay for a book again! Heaven knows I've already downloaded more books than I'd be able to read in three lifetimes. But there's two things I've never been able to refuse—free food and free books.

Of the thousands of new books made available every day, I whittle the list down to highlight only the best on Kindle Buffet . For this, I use a two simple yardsticks: how many five-star reviews have Amazon customers posted about the book? Then, to skim the cream a bit more, I compare a book's number of positive reviews versus negative reviews. Although individual reviewers frequently disagree about a given book—and Amazon certainly has its share of knuckleheads offering their two-cents' worth—the bottom line is usually clear: the best, most widely enjoyed books attract the most (and best percentage of) positive reviews.

Kindle Buffet also has bestseller lists, updated hourly, of free Kindle books for every Amazon category—fiction, romance, business, cookbooks—you name it. So if you'd like to load up your Kindle with plenty of great reading material without spending a dime, visit KindleBuffet.com.

Browsing and Buying Music

Browsing and buying music is easy on a Kindle Fire. Like any other purchases you make, digital media you buy from Amazon will remain in the Cloud until you choose to download it to your devices. (You can also load your own music onto the device using a Mini USB cable, as explained in the section in Chapter 1, **Using a Mini USB Connection to Transfer Content**).

To access your Music library:

1. Select the **Music** link on the top menu of your **home-screen**.
2. You'll be taken to your **Library** of music.
3. Select "**Store >**"

You'll be taken to the following screen.

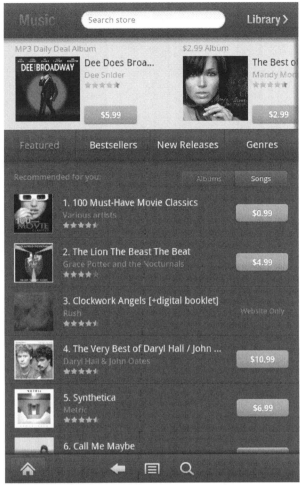

Figure 35: The Amazon music store

You can search for a particular artist or album using the search field at the top of the screen. Once you click on an entry, you'll be taken to a summary screen providing information on the album and purchasing options.

Figure 36: Summary of the album '100 Must-Have Movie Classics'.

Here's something about buying music on Amazon you'll probably like: Have you ever wanted to buy just one song from an album, instead of the whole thing? Now you can. Notice that each track on the "100 Must-Have Movie Classics" album shown above has an individual price of 99 cents. If you wish, you can buy one song off of the album and skip the rest. No more wasted money on songs you never wanted! Also, you can sample a song before deciding whether to buy it. The buttons on the left side of the song titles allow you to listen to part of the song free.

TIP: There is a 1/8" headphone jack on the bottom of your Kindle Fire. Here you can connect a pair of stereo headphones or external speakers to enhance your listening pleasure. You can also use the jack to connect your Kindle's audio to many home theaters and other music players.

Browsing and Buying Video

When you purchase digital video through Amazon, you're not limited to viewing the video on your Kindle. If you wish, you can also view the same content on a desktop computer. Some newer TVs also support Amazon's streaming video service.

Here's how to watch video content on your Kindle:

1. Select "**Video**" from the **home-screen** menu
2. Select **Store** >from the **Library** interface

You'll see this screen:

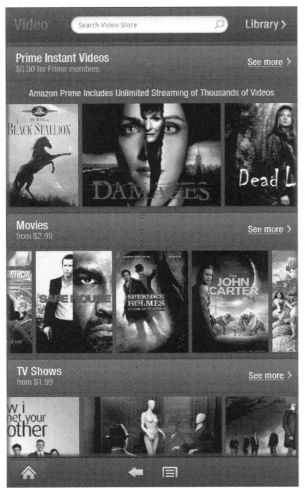

Figure 37: The Amazon video store.

Click on a movie or television show and you'll get a summary screen, pictured below:

Figure 38: A movie summary screen.

From here, you can add the movie to your Watch-list—which is essentially a favorites list—or you can watch it immediately. The Black Stallion happens to be included free with an Amazon Prime membership. If you were looking at a summary for a movie that was not included with the service, you would have the option to purchase the movie.

Briefly: Two ways of buying streaming video

Amazon provides two options for buying streaming video: You can purchase it outright, or you can rent it. If you purchase a video, you're free to stream it whenever you want from any compatible device. You can download the video to any compatible device to watch it at your leisure when you're offline, but it may only be stored on two devices at once. On the other hand, if you choose to rent a video, you'll have 24 hours to finish watching it.

Videos offered free through Amazon Prime are handled differently. With a Prime membership, you can stream these videos whenever you want and however many times you want. You cannot, however, download them for storage on your device—unless you actually purchase the video.

Here's a recap on the three options for buying video:

- **Buy a Video:** Stream whenever you want, download to as many as two devices at once.
- **Rent a Video:** Watch it within 24-hours. The video may not be downloaded.

- **Prime Videos:** Stream anytime, as often as you wish. But you can't download it for storage on your device unless you purchase it outright.

TIP: If you have young children in your home, it's best to supervise their use of video on the Kindle. If One-Click purchasing is enabled—and your Kindle has no Parental Controls enabled—children can run up quite a tab without understanding the cost of video purchases.

Videos that you download to your Kindle will appear in your Library, just as is the case with other media.

Searching for and Downloading Apps

Apps provide your Kindle Fire with many different functionalities. Your Kindle Fire is set up to download and install applications from the Amazon App Store. This process is remarkably easy and fast.

TIP: There are 3rd party apps out there that you can get from other sources. It's safest to get your Apps from Amazon to avoid any problems with your Kindle Fire.

To get to your Apps:

1. Click on the **App** link at the top of your **home-screen.**
2. Select any App's icon to open it

TIP: Some Apps are really just shortcuts to websites. For example, the Facebook App simply opens up your Silk web browser to Facebook's website for mobile devices, M.Facebook.com. Other apps, however, have more advanced functionalities built in. The imo App, for example, allows you to connect with several different instant-messaging services.

My App library is shown below. Notice it has a similar look and feel as the other libraries on the Kindle Fire.

Figure 39: App library.

Note that "**Cloud**" is selected on the top of the screen. This means that my Kindle is displaying all the Apps to which I have access, even the ones I haven't yet downloaded and installed on my device. Those apps that aren't yet installed on my Kindle are designated by the downward-pointing arrow superimposed on their icons.

Select "**Store >**" to go to the App store. You'll see a screen similar to the one pictured in Figure 40. Each day, Amazon Prime members are allowed to download a paid app for free. Note that there are different categories shown at the top of the list of Apps. This allows you to browse them more efficiently.

You can search for Apps by using the search field at the top of the screen.

TIP: You can search for Apps by function, as well as by title. For instance, XiiaLive Lite is an MP3 stream player. You can find it by searching for it by name or by searching for a phrase related to its function, such as "MP3 stream player."

Figure 40: The Amazon App Store.

Briefly: Know your Android

e Kindle Fire is an Android-based device, which enables you to access thousands of apps originally developed for use on smartphones. Unfortunately, not all Android Apps function as advertised, and some of them can even be dangerous. The good thing about Amazon's App Store is that everything listed there has been screened and approved by Amazon's staff.

Installing an App

Installing apps is very easy. Click on the name of the App you want and you'll get a description of it. The description may contain general information, photos, reviews and recommendations, although some Apps, particularly those that aren't very popular, have less information included in their summary pages.

In **Figure 41**, below, you can see the summary page for the CNET News App:

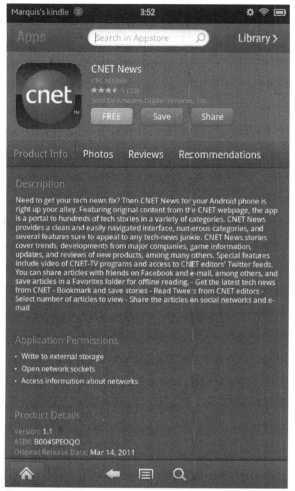

Figure 41: The summary page for the CNET News app.

This particular app is free, so it has a button indicating this right alongside it. Select that button and the text will change to "Get App" and the button color turns green. Select "Get App," and the download and installation happens automatically—assuming, of course, you have a Wi-Fi connection.

How Many Apps Can You Have?

The number of apps you can have on your device is limited by the amount of storage capacity you have dedicated to them on the Kindle Fire. By default, this is a little more than 1GB. To find out how much space you have available, do the following:

1. Go to your **home-screen.**
2. Click on the **Gear Icon** in your **Status Bar.**
3. Click on "**More....**
4. Click on "**Device.**"
5. You'll see the following screen:

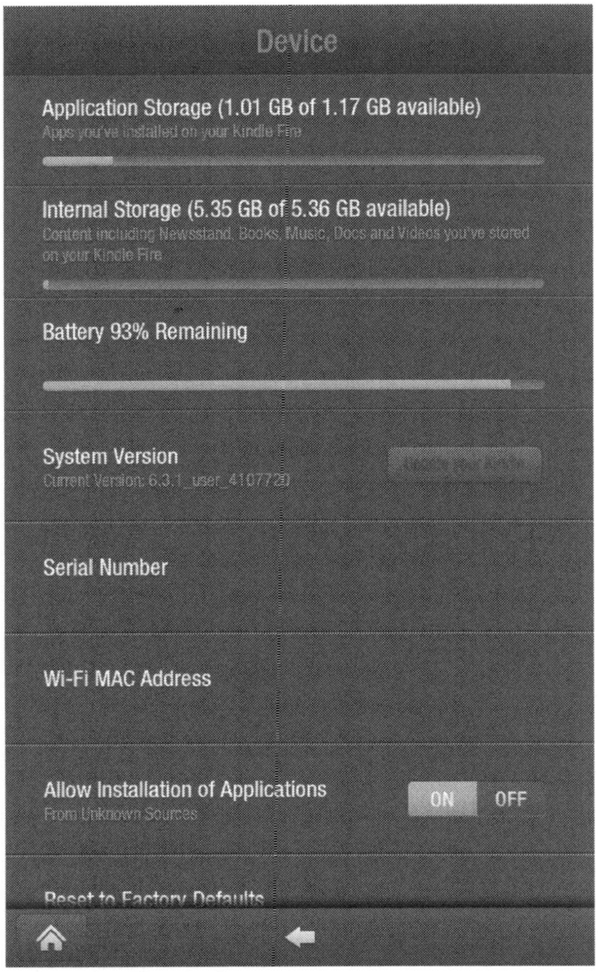

Figure 42: The device screen

The orange bar underneath the words **Application Storage** shows you how much space you have remaining on your Kindle Fire for Apps. Note that your **Internal Storage** is counted differently and that it applies specifically to media content, including books, videos, and so forth.

Look at the toggle for "Allow Installation of Applications From Unknown Sources". Setting this to "**On**", as mine is, allows you to install Apps from sources other than the Amazon App store. If you're planning on using Apps that come from other sources, you'll need this toggled to "**On.**"

Removing Apps

Removing apps can be done in two different ways. The first simply removes the App from your device, but leaves it in the Amazon Cloud so it's available for downloading again later. Considering the amount of storage you get with the Amazon Cloud—and the small size of most apps—this is a sensible option.

To remove an App and leave it in the Amazon Cloud:

1. On your **home-screen** click "**Apps**"
2. Click "**Device**" on top of the **App Library**
3. Press and hold the icon for the **App** you want to remove
4. Select "**Remove from Device**" from the pop-up menu

Figure 43: Removing an app.

This will send the App back into the Amazon Cloud, freeing up space on your device. Note that some apps come pre-installed on the Kindle Fire, and can't be removed. You can remove them from your Favorites, which means they won't appear in your library, but they remain on your device. The good news: most of these default apps are merely Internet shortcuts, such as IMDb, so they consume very little storage space.

To Permanently Delete an App

If you want to delete an App permanently, you'll have to do so from your account page at Amazon.com:

1. Navigate to Amazon.com/myk and log in
2. Select "**Manage Your Apps**" from the "**Other Digital Content**" menu
3. Find the App you want to get rid of on the list
4. Click on the "**Actions**" dropdown menu on the right of the App name
5. Select "**Delete this App**" from the menu

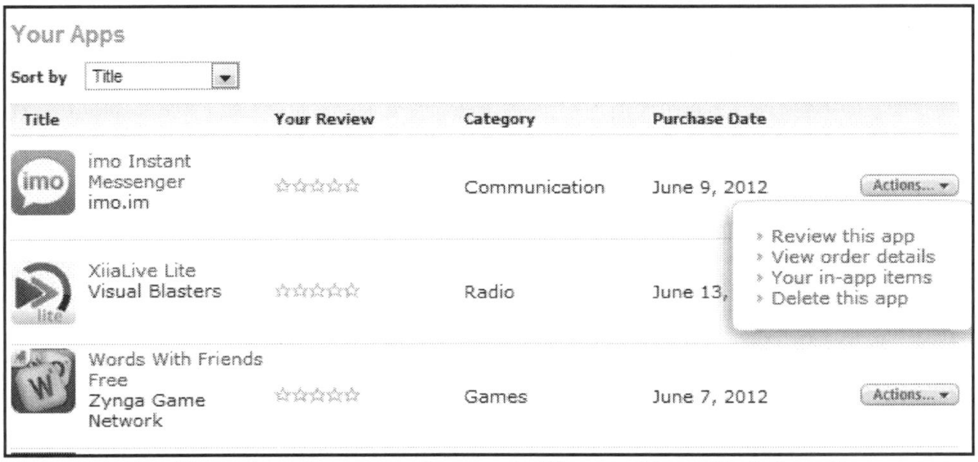

Figure 44: The 'Your Apps' page on Amazon's 'Manage Your Kindle' section.

TIP: Once you delete an App entirely in the manner just described, it's gone for good. If you want to reinstall it on your Kindle, you must purchase it again. Remember, you have plenty of room for storage in the Amazon Cloud. Even if you've tired of an application, keep it in the Cloud if there's a chance you might use it again.

In-App Items

In-App items are additional items offered from app publishers. For example, some "free" game apps contain premium features that may only be accessed after purchasing the in-app item. Some games allow you to play up to a certain level, then require a purchase before you can advance to the next level.

As usual, you purchase In-App items via your One-Click settings. If you don't have Parental Controls enabled on your Kindle, this is another opportunity for children to inadvertently spend a lot of your money. Here's how to prevent such accidents:

1. Go to your **home-screen.**
2. Click the **Gear Icon** to bring up your settings.
3. Select "**More….**"
4. Go to **Parental Controls.**
5. Toggle the selector to "**On.**"
6. Set your password.
7. Select **Block and Unblock Content Types.**
8. Toggle the entry next to **Apps** to switch it to **Blocked.**

As you can see, shopping with the Kindle Fire easy. It's designed to make shopping for digital content as smooth as possible.

Believe it or not, so far we've merely scratched the surface of your Kindle Fire's capabilities. In the next chapter, you'll discover how to use your web browser to do many of the tasks you've previously been able to handle only with a desktop or laptop computer.

4 ▶ USING KINDLE FIRE TO SURF THE WEB

One of the best features of the Kindle Fire is how well its designed for portable web browsing. The Fire's "Silk" browser harnesses your device's processor and Amazon's Cloud to make your Internet experience as fast and smooth as possible. Don't hesitate to tilt your Kindle over to landscape orientation, which often makes typing and navigating the web easier.

Navigating the Web with the Silk Browser

Getting on the Internet couldn't be easier. Go to your **home-screen** and select **Web** from the navigation menu. This will launch the browser:

Figure 45: The Silk browser opened to Google.com.

The first time you open up your browser, you'll see a set of bookmarks. These come preset in the browser and include some of the most commonly visited websites. Just tap one of these bookmarks and you'll arrive at the corresponding page. This screen will include your history as you browse the Internet. For example, if you've recently visited Facebook using the Silk browser, that site will become one of the icons that appear on this initial screen.

To navigate to a web page, enter the address in the URL bar. When you start to type in an address, you'll list will appear. This will contain bookmarked pages, your history and suggestions for searches. The bookmarks are denoted by the bookmark icon, the history entries are denoted by a clock icon and the search suggestions by a magnifying glass icon. Tap any one of these to take the related action.

Tabbed browsing is a feature of the Silk browser. To open a new tab, click on the "+" sign on the top of the browser, pictured below in **Figure 46**. See **Figure 45** for the exact position of the + symbol on your browser window.

Figure 46: The '+' Sign opens a new browser tab. In this illustration, tapping the 'X' sign would close the browser tab showing Google.com.

Having numerous browser tabs open simultaneously will gradually degrade your browser's speed, but you can have several open without noticing much of a difference. To switch between tabs, simply tap the appropriate tab, and that tab will move to the front.

Zoom In or Out

To get a closer look at a website, you can zoom in by tapping on the center of the screen. This automatically resizes the page so that the main portion fills your screen. Another way to zoom in (or out) is by spreading or "pinching" two fingers along the touch-screen. Here's how: to zoom in, place two of your fingers in the center of the screen and then spread them apart, moving your fingers toward the edges of the screen. You might think of this gesture as grabbing onto the webpage and stretching it outward. Practice this a couple of times to get a feel for it. The opposite gesture—an inward, pinching motion— enables you to zoom out.

Reading View

Reading View is a great option for many web pages. You access it by clicking the **Glasses** icon on the bottom menu bar of your Silk browser. Note the difference in the figures below.

Figure 47: Normal View. Note the glasses econ on the right side of the bottom menu bar.

Obviously, the text in the illustration above is too small for most folks to read. One option for magnifying the text is with the finger gestures we just discussed—but that might not work because in some cases, by zooming in you won't be able to view the whole column of text—you'd have to scroll from side to side to read each line, and that would be a tedious chore indeed. Also, because you need to continue scrolling down to advance through the text, you may end up touching a hyperlink in the text, and inadvertently navigating away from the page you're trying to read. The solution is to use the **Reading View** feature accessible with the glasses icon. This convenient feature neatly reformats the web page into a eBook-like display. Here's how to do it:

Click on the **Glasses Icon**, pictured below to open **Reading View**, pictured in **Figure 49**.

Figure 48: The glasses icon opens Reading View.

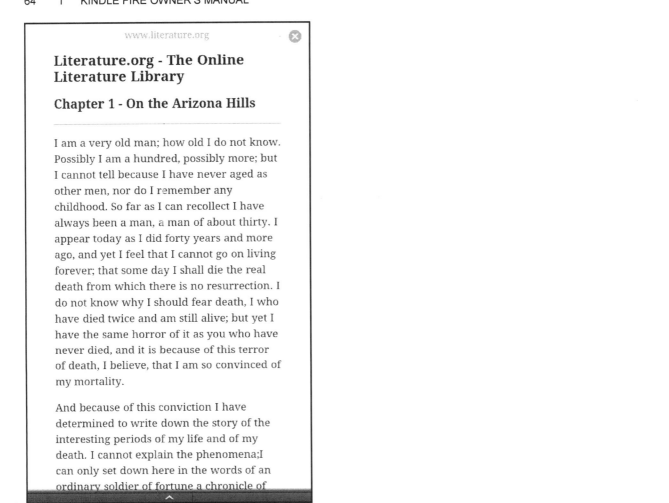

Figure 49: Reading View of the text from Figure 47. To exit Reading View, tap the 'X' in the upper right-hand corner.

Doesn't that look better? Big, bold text and generous line spacing—and the removal of all the distractions from the webpage—enables you to read the passage comfortably. Any time you encounter a web page with lots of text you want to read, switching to **Reading View** is usually the best way to proceed.

TIP: Pages with images that are part of the text will display with those images in Reading View. This makes it a lot more enjoyable to read news stories.

Bookmarking Web Pages

Bookmarking web pages is easy. When you're at a URL that you want to bookmark, hit the **Bookmark** icon, which is pictured in **Figure 47**. You can see where it's located on your browser in **Figure 45**.

Figure 50: The Bookmark icon.

Once you tap the **Bookmark** icon, you'll be taken to the page of predefined bookmarks. The page you selected will appear as an icon on the upper left-hand side of the screen and will have a "+" sign superimposed on it. Simply tap this icon to create the bookmark.

TIP: You can access your existing bookmarks by tapping the **Bookmark** icon, as well. The page you're on will still show up with the + sign over it, but you can go to any of your bookmarks by simply tapping on the appropriate icon.

Searching the Web

If you're getting the idea that the Silk browser makes everything really easy ... well, you're right. Searching the web is easy on this browser, too. Google.com is bookmarked by default and is perhaps the most obvious choice for your search page.

Google's predictive search feature will cause a dropdown list of probable options to appear as you're typing in text. For instance, once I typed in "A Princess of" into the search field, the dropdown showed "A Princess of Mars Movie" as the likely option. Pretty cool. Most of the time, you don't even have to hit the "**Go**" or Google search button. The search you want will be performed as soon as you finish entering some text. You can tap on any predictive result to select it.

Figure 51: Google's Predictive Search Feature.

Take a look at **Figure 52** and notice a couple of things.

1. The keyboard has a "**Go**" button on it in orange. You can tap this to search instead of hitting the magnifying glass next to the search field.
2. You have two different navigation bars. One is provided by the Google web page. It contains the words "**Web**", "**Images**", "**Videos**" and "**More >**". The other is just below the URL bar and starts with the word "**+You**". The upper bar is for your Google services, the lower is a standard feature of the webpage.

Figure 52: The Google search page in Silk.

TIP: If the keyboard disappears, tap the search field again. The keyboard will surface.

Searching any site with its own search field works exactly the same, minus the features specific to Google, of course.

Searching from the URL Bar

You can also search directly from the URL bar. Simply type in your search terms and you'll be presented with a list of predictive results. You can see how the predictive results feature looks from the URL bar in **Figure 53**, below.

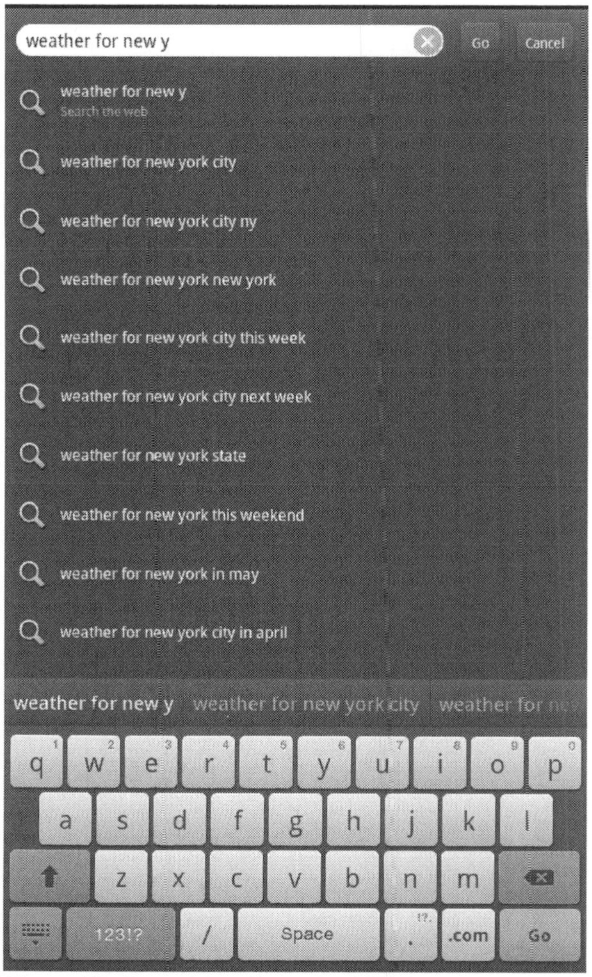

Figure 53: Searching from the URL bar on the Silk browser.

To see any of the predictive results pages, tap the appropriate text and you'll be taken to the Google results page for those terms. To type in a search that isn't listed among the predictive results, finish typing it in the URL bar and tap "**Go**" beside the entry itself or press the keyboard's **Go** button.

Browser Options/Settings

You can access your browser settings by tapping the **Menu** button, shown below.

Figure 54: The Menu button appears in the middle of the bar at the bottom of your browser.

Tap this button and you'll see the following menu surface at the bottom of your screen:

Figure 55: The Browser options menu.

Tap the "**Settings**" entry to get to the following screen.

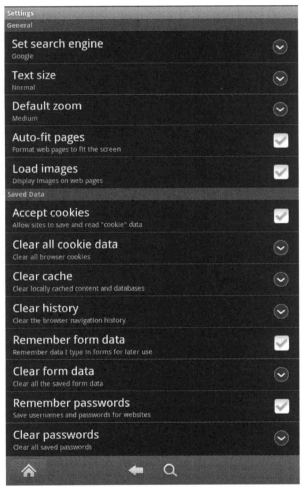

Figure 56: The Expanded Browser settings menu.

The **Browser Settings** menu includes the following options and settings. Scroll down the screen to see the complete list:

- Set Search Engine
- Text Size
- Default Zoom
- Auto-Fit Pages
- Load Images

- Accept Cookies
- Clear All Cookie Data
- Clear Cache
- Clear History
- Remember Form Data
- Clear Form Data
- Remember Passwords
- Clear Passwords
- Show Security Warnings
- Enable Flash
- Enable JavaScript
- Open Pages in Overview
- Open in background
- Block Pop-Up Windows
- Accelerate Page Loading
- Optional Encryption
- Desktop of Mobile View
- Text Encoding
- Website Settings
- Reset to Default

Simply tap on any of the settings named above to change them. Some settings are self-explanatory, but some require special consideration:

Privacy Settings/Options

Several of the web browser settings are security-related. The **Remember Passwords** setting, for instance, determines whether the browser will automatically fill in your password on restricted sites. If you're worried about security, be sure to set this to "off." Uncheck the box by tapping on it to turn **Remember Passwords** off.

Optional Encryption is another setting related to security. It renders data unreadable to third parties when it's being sent to and from Amazon's Cloud servers. If you're using public Wi-Fi networks, it's prudent to turn this on by checking the box—although it may slow down your Internet connection somewhat. The encryption is provided via SSL (Secure Sockets Layer). This is not the same type of encryption as you'd get from a VPN (Virtual Private Network) service. It applies only to the traffic that goes from your device to the Amazon Cloud servers.

Privacy and the Cloud

Many Kindle Fire users are concerned about a privacy tradeoff made necessary by using the Silk browser with Amazon's cloud. To make the system work as fast as possible, Amazon needs to know which websites you're visiting. The Cloud allows you to browse faster by pushing common website to your device, but some Kindle Fire users are concerned about Amazon having a record of their web activity. Here are the facts:

1. The Amazon Cloud doesn't associate your web page history with your device.

2. Crash reports are sometimes sent from your device to the cloud. This may contain identifying information, such as your IP address and your MAC address.

Turning Off the Cloud

If you're uncomfortable about Amazon being able to see your Internet history, you can avoid going through the Amazon Cloud, and if you have a speedy Wi-Fi connection, you might not notice any sluggishness in web browsing. Here's how to change the setting:

1. Open your **Browser Settings**
2. Pull the screen up until you see "**Accelerate page loading**"
3. Uncheck the box
4. If you have **Optional Encryption** enabled, this option will grey out once you change the Cloud preferences

See Figure 57 to verify that you've disconnected from the cloud:

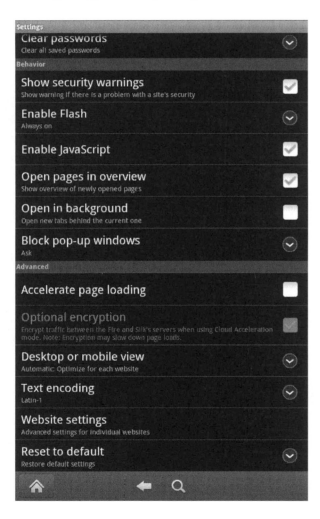

Figure 57: The Silk browser with 'accelerated page loading (the Amazon Cloud) turned off.

Remember to clear your **History** if you want to keep your browsing confidential and if someone else has access to your Kindle Fire. Your Kindle Fire, with the Amazon Cloud turned off, functions just as does any other Internet browsing device in terms of privacy and security.

Viewing email on your Kindle Fire

You have two options for accessing email on your Kindle Fire—through the Silk web browser or using the preloaded Email app. Here's how to use the app:

1. Open the **Email App** from your **App Library.**

2. Select your email provider to proceed with the setup. If you have a Pop-3 email service, select "Other." See Figure 58.

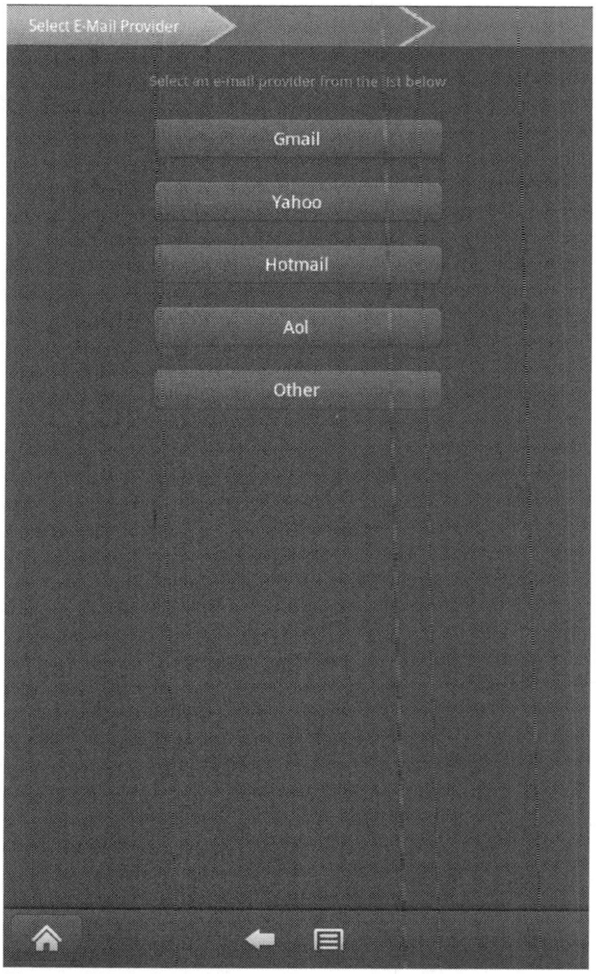

Figure 58: Select your provider from the list.

The next screen requests your username and password. Enter them, then click "**Next.**" Note that "**Next**" appears on the bottom of your keyboard. You can use this button—or you can use the regular button at the bottom of the setup screen; the both do the same job.

TIP: If you use your Kindle Fire for viewing email, you should consider requiring a password to awaken your Kindle. Otherwise, anyone who picks up your Kindle could view your personal messages.

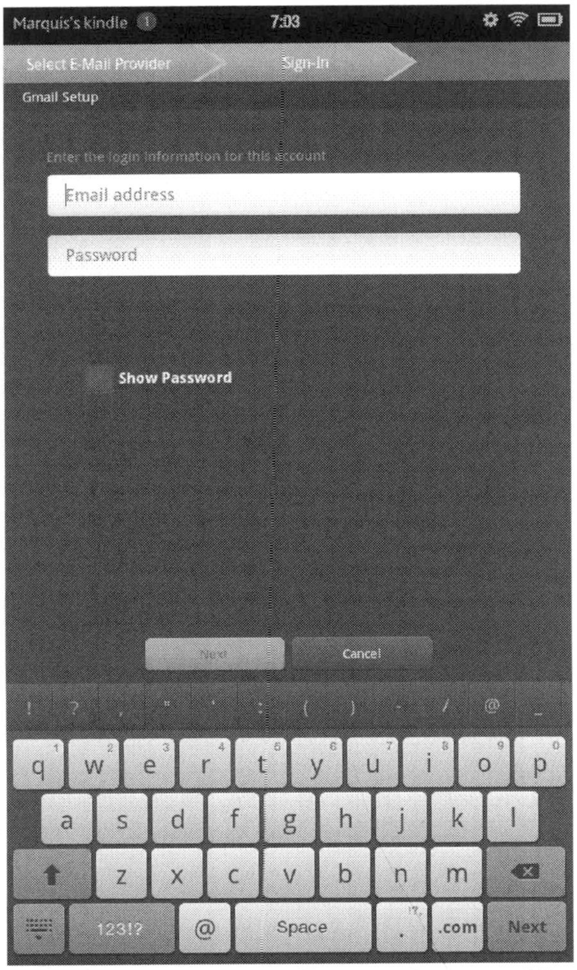

Figure 59: The Username/Password screen of the Email app.

After you've completed these fields, you'll be asked to enter the name that should appear in the "From" field of your email messages. And you'll be asked to name the account. If you use more than one email account, you should assign unique names to each.

Now you've completed your email setup.

TIP: You'll receive a visual cue in the upper-left corner of your screen when you receive new email messages. The number of new messages is represented by a circled numeral next to your name. If you also want your Kindle Fire to provide an audible alert when new messages arrive, you'll need to ensure that "notification sounds" are enabled from the menu **Device Settings (Gear Icon>...More).**

To access the Email app, you'll need to visit your **Apps Library.** If you frequently view email using your Kindle Fire, you might wish to add the Email app to your **Favorites** part of your home-screen. Just press and hold the icon for the app and it will show up on the **Favorites** shelf below your carousel.

5 ▶ HOW TO READ A BOOK, KINDLE STYLE

When most people think of a "Kindle," they think of an eReader. Before the Fire came along, that's about all you could do with an eReader—read books. Back then, most eReaders came with a black-and-white display called E-ink. The older models—which are still quite popular—don't emit any light. The Kindle Fire, however, functions more like a computer monitor—generating its own light of varying colors. The reading experience is quite different, but the Fire functions quite nicely as an eReader. And although there are zillions of Kindle eBooks from which to choose, they're only the tip of the iceberg when it comes to reading on your Kindle

Using Kindle's Personal Documents Service

One of the strongest features of the Kindle Fire is its compact size. It's easy to tote around and, if you wish, it can take the place of a laptop computer. If you're going to use your Fire frequently as an eReader or productivity tool, taking advantage of Amazon's Personal Documents Service is a must. Although Amazon's Kindle books use a proprietary format—you need a Kindle (or a Kindle app) to read them—you can send virtually any kind of digital document to your Kindle using the Personal Documents Service.

You can use the Personal Documents Service along with your Send-to-Kindle email address. The email address is usually formatted as follows:

[Your Name]@Kindle.com

If you're unsure of your Send-to-Kindle address, you can review it at Amazon's "Manage Your Kindle" web page, Amazon.com/myk.

Before you can actually use the document service, you'll need to approve the use of the Send-to-Kindle email address. We'll take care of that right now:

1. Visit Amazon.com/myk and log in
2. On the left hand side of the screen, you'll see "**Personal Document Settings.**" Click on that link.
3. Under the pop-up labeled "**Add a new approved e-mail address,**" enter the desired address and click "**Add Address.**" The screen is pictured below:

Figure 60: Adding an email address to the Personal Document Service list at Amazon's 'Manage Your Kindle' page.

Note that the regular email address registered with your Amazon account is already added to the approved list.

Briefly: Keeping a lid on @Kindle

Be very selective about what email addresses you add to this "approved" list. The last thing you want on your Kindle is spam. If you have friends with a penchant for forwarding humorous emails, you might not want that on your Kindle either. Instead of giving out your Kindle address—or adding friends' addresses to your "approved" list, just forward any important documents to your @Kindle address yourself.

Now, let's actually send a document to see how it works. Most text or photo documents work fine (a complete list of compatible formats appears in Chapter 1 of this book). You can attach up to 25 documents to a single email, but their combined size must not exceed 50 megabytes.

Attach a document to an email and send it to your Kindle address, address ([Your Name]@Kindle.com). Leave the subject line of the email blank if you wish.

You can send the document from any Internet-connected device.

After you've sent your document, you have two options for storing it. You can archive it on your Kindle (in which case it will be accessible without Wi-Fi) or you can store it in the Cloud. Documents sent to your Kindle appear on your **Docs** bookshelf.

TIP: If your document doesn't appear on your device promptly, tap the **Sync** button in your **Gear Icon** menu. It can take a few minutes for the document to arrive.

Converting documents. One of the best features of the Personal Documents Service is that it can automatically convert most common document formats to the Kindle format, called AZW. You don't have to know the technical details, it just works. Then once the document is on your Kindle, you can use many of the functions available with Kindle documents—you can make annotations, change the font, adjust the text size, and so forth. To convert your documents, enter the word "Convert" in the subject line of the email.

TIP: Don't use Personal Documents Service for commercial purposes, such as sending out a commercial newsletter. It's against Amazon's terms of service, and that's why it's called the **Personal Documents Service.**

Using the 'Send-to-Kindle' application on your computer

There's an alternative to the Send-to-Kindle email method that's even easier to use, especially if you forward many documents from your computer to your Kindle. Free software provided by Amazon, called the "Send-to-Kindle application," is available for PCs and Macs. You can download it here:

Windows PCs: www.amazon.com/sendtokindle/pc
Macintosh: www.amazon.com/sendtokindle/mac

When you launch the software for the first time, you'll be asked for Amazon username and password.

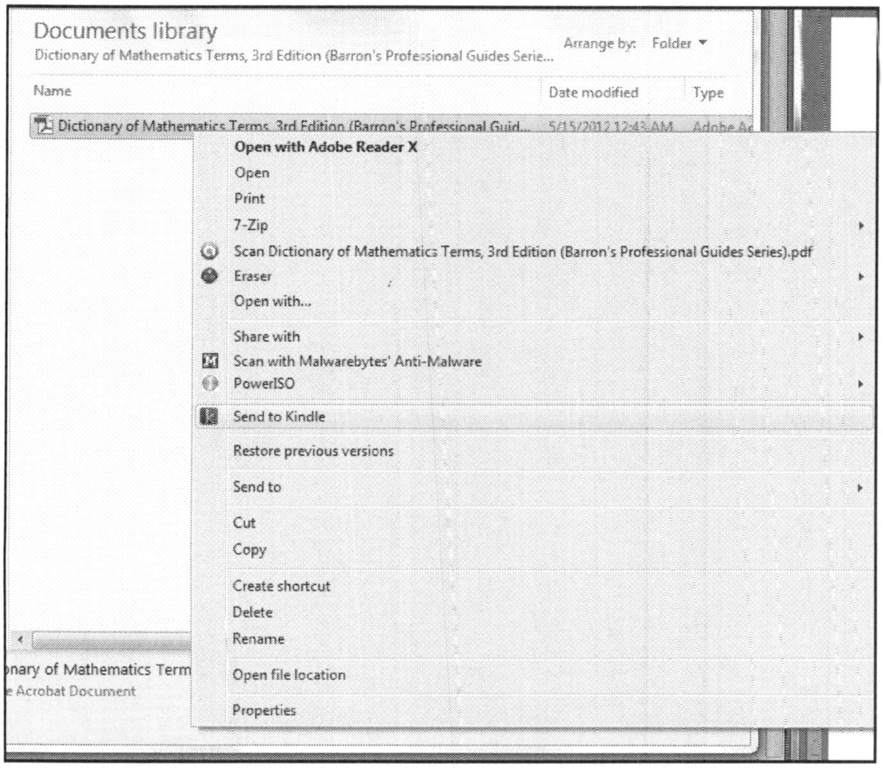

Figure 61: Sending a document to Kindle using the Send-to-Kindle app using Windows.

The Send-to-Kindle application is quite efficient and easy to use, and it automatically converts documents to the Kindle format. After installing it on your computer, it offers two methods of sending documents. First, using your mouse, right-click on your document as illustrated in Figure 61 below. You'll see a right-click menu with the option to "send to Kindle."

Your second option for sending documents is to use the regular "print" command while viewing your document. But instead of selecting your printer from the menu, you'll select "Send to Kindle."

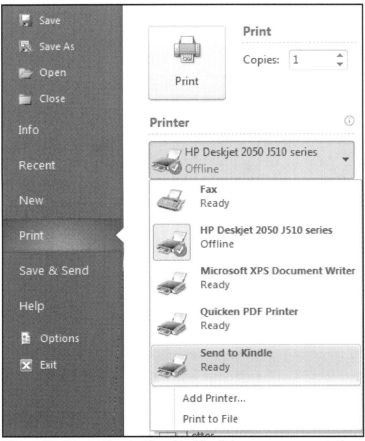

Figure 62: The option to 'Send to Kindle' appears as a printing option after installation of the Send-to-Kindle' app.

Send to Kindle will be added as a printer option in office programs and other software that allows printing.

TIP: We'll delve into more details about converting documents to the Kindle format in Chapter 10. For now, suffice to say that if you want to be able to manage your document like a Kindle eBook, convert your document before sending it to your device.

Using the Books 'Library'

Yet another cool feature of the Kindle is the potential for borrowing and lending Kindle eBooks. Specifically, you can:

- Borrow books from your local library, when available, or;
- Lend books to friends and colleagues from your Kindle.

Remember the days when you'd loan your printed books to friends, and (depending on the friend) rarely see the book again? Well, a great feature of lending books via your Kindle is that all your books will actually be returned—there's no way around it. Loans are capped at 14 days by Amazon's system.

Not all Kindle books are eligible for lending—the publisher has to agree to the program. When you're shopping for Kindle books nowadays, you'll see a notation—whether lending is "enabled" or not—in the "Product Details" of the book's listing on Amazon.

TIP: Remember, you can loan Kindle books to virtually anyone with an email address, regardless of whether they have a Kindle device. Kindle reading apps are available free for practically every type of computer, smartphone, and other digital gadgets.

Here's the procedure for lending a Kindle book:

1. Visit the "Manage Your Kindle" page, Amazon.com/myk.
2. Click on the "**Actions**" button on the right-hand side of the title you wish to lend. In the pop-up menu, select "Loan this title."

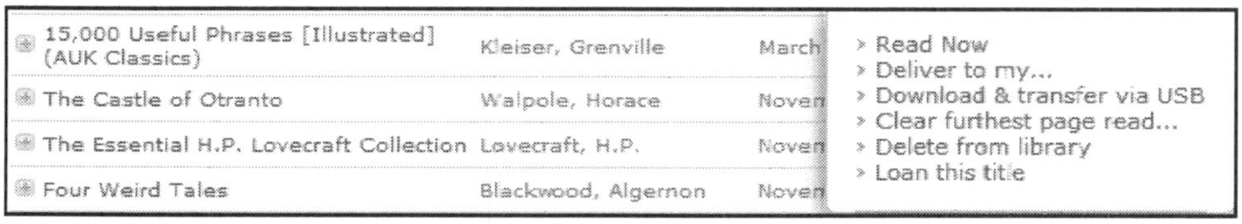

Figure 63: Select "Loan this title" to Get to the Next Step.

Next you'll arrive at this screen:

Figure 64: Lending Details.

Simply complete the form, and your friend will receive the book. It will be returned to your library automatically in 14 days or, if the borrower finishes the book before then, it can be returned early. Remember, while your book is being borrowed, you won't have access to it on your Kindle.

Unfortunately, you may loan a Kindle book only once—that is Amazon's current policy. But I would not be surprised if the lending program, which is relatively new, is amended to be more lenient in the future.

Borrowing Kindle books from a library. You can also use your Kindle to borrow eBooks from public libraries, as long as the facility offers a digital lending service—and a great many do so nowadays. If you're unsure whether your local library offers Kindle books, visit http://Search.Overdrive.com. OverDrive is the name of the service libraries use to administer Kindle lending.

Compared to the old days, borrowing books from the library is mighty convenient. For one thing, with your Kindle, you don't have to travel to the library to find and borrow a book. Also, you don't need to remember to return it. With Kindle editions, the fines for overdue books are a distant memory.

Here's how to borrow a Kindle book from a library:

1. Visit your library's website.
2. Search for the Kindle book you want. EBooks are usually listed in a separate section than printed books.
3. If the book is available, check it out—or place a hold on the title.
4. You may have to enter your library card number.
5. When prompted for your email address, provide your regular address, not your @Kindle address.
6. If available, you'll be given an option to **Get for Kindle**. Select that option.

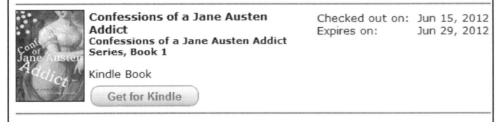

Figure 65: Selecting 'Get for Kindle' from a library website.

7. You'll be taken to the **Amazon Public Library Loan** page
8. Click on the "**Deliver to**" menu and select "**Get library book**"

TIP: Due to the anti-copying restrictions used by some publishers, not all Kindle books available through libraries can be transferred wirelessly—sometimes a physical connection with a USB cord is required. But you can obtain software for transferring the books via USB from OverDrive at http://www.overdrive.com/software/omc/. You might also want to review the procedure for transferring content to your Kindle via USB in Chapter 1 of this book.

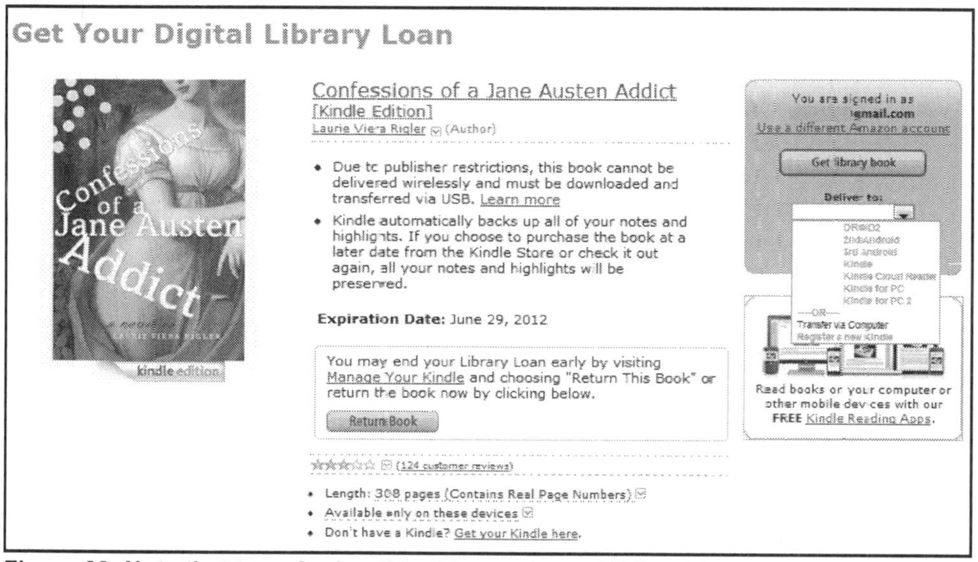

Figure 66: Note that transferring this title requires a USB cable.

If you finish the book before the expiration date, you may return it early via the **Manage Your Kindle** page.

Like other digital items, Kindle books—including those you borrow—can be added to your "Favorites" by tapping and holding on their icon. This adds a shortcut to the book at the bottom of your Kindle's home-screen , allowing quick access.

Navigating books and documents

Ah, the virtues of the eBook—they're convenient, easy on the environment, and a lot of fun. But that's only the beginning. EBooks enable you to combine computing horsepower with your own reading skills, opening vast new horizons for learning and literature appreciation. Let's explore some of the possibilities.

Basic EBook Navigation. If you've used your Kindle Fire for a while, navigating eBooks is a cinch, but let's recap it quickly:

- To advance a page forward, "pull" the page starting at the right-hand side of the screen. Or simply tap the right-hand side of the screen.
- To move a page backward, "pull" the page starting at the left-hand side of the screen or tap the left-hand side of the screen.

To navigate to specific sections of the book, tap the center of the screen to bring up the options bar, which enables you to:

- Go **Home.**
- Go **Back.**

- Change the **Font Settings**.
- Pull up the **Menu.**
- **Share** comments via social networking.
- **Search** for a word or passage.
- Use a **Slider** to navigate to a specific page.

The menu appears like this:

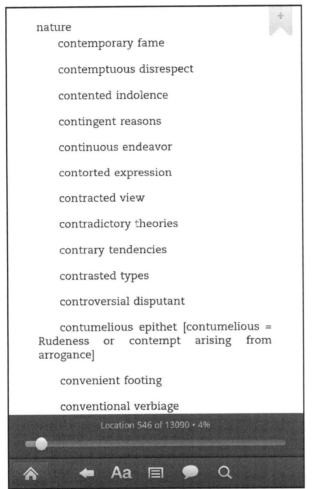

Figure 67: The EBook Navigation Menu. The Slider is on top. On the lower menu from left to right: Home, Back, Font, Menu, Comment, Search.

Whenever you need to advance or regress more than a few pages, the slider (the bar near the bottom of your screen) is a handy feature. It works a lot better than trying to move page-by-page—if you rapidly tap the screen several times, it's hard to see which page you're on.

TIP: With eBooks, "page numbers" have taken on a whole new meaning (or perhaps they've lost their meaning entirely). For example, let's imagine you're writing a research paper, and you're citing a book as a reference. For any given passage in the book, the page number shown on your Kindle Fire will be different than the page number in printed editions. So, in your citation, be sure to specify that you're referring to the eBook. As an example, the book pictured in **Figure 67**, "15,000 Useful Phrases" usually has less than 300 pages in printed editions. But the Kindle edition has more than 13,000 "pages" simply because there are fewer words shown on each page. Also, if you adjust the font or text size, the Kindle edition's page count will change. In fact, your Kindle will refer to a numbered "location" in a book, in an attempt to be more precise than a "page number." Meanwhile, competing systems—such as books published through Apple's iBookstore and those available through Barnes & Noble's "Nook"—attempt to refer to page numbers in printed editions. The trouble is, are they referring to the paperback or the hardback? The first edition, or the second? One thing is for sure—it's a whole new can of worms.

Searching within books

Finding a needle in a haystack is as easy as falling off a log—if you're using your Kindle. The Search button, represented by the magnifying-glass icon on the right side of the menu shown in **Figure 67**, allows you to search for words or phrases. Here's how to perform a search:

1. Tap the center of the screen to call up the menu.
2. Tap the **Magnifying Glass**.
3. Use the keyboard to enter your term(s) in the search field on the top of the screen.
4. Tap "**Go**" on the keyboard or the **Magnifying Glass** next to the search field.

Remember that the search function will find every single instance of the term or phrase you specify. If you search for a common word like "the," for instance, you'll get bogged down with a ton of references.

The search function is quite handy when you're using reference books, and it's smart too. For example, if you were searching for the word "antidisestablishmentarianism," you needn't type the whole thing. Just type "antidisest," and your target will show up.

To navigate from the search results to the text location where the word actually occurs, just tap the appropriate display in the search results.

Bookmarking and highlighting

Whether you're reading for pleasure or studying for a school assignment, the Kindle's bookmarking and highlighting features are great tools.

For example, imagine you're taking a class on English Literature. And your instructor wants you to determine the origin of the familiar expression, "band of brothers." Using paper books, this is a chore—you might need to thumb through every doggone page of Shakespeare's *King Henry V.* until you hit paydirt, the St. Crispin's Day speech in Scene III. By then, you might have fallen asleep. But with the Kindle, it's dead easy—you just search, then scan your results. First, you'd search for "band of brothers" using the procedure mentioned a few paragraphs above. Then you'd see the following screen (which might look a bit different, depending on which edition of The Bard's works you're using).

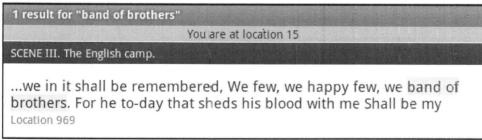

1 result for "band of brothers"

You are at location 15

SCENE III. The English camp.

...we in it shall be remembered, We few, we happy few, we band of brothers. For he to-day that sheds his blood with me Shall be my

Location 969

Figure 68: Search results for "band of brothers" in Henry V by Shakespeare.

Tap on any of the search results, and you'll be taken to the appropriate page, where the entry will be highlighted.

To **Highlight** the selection so you'll be able to easily reference it in the future, tap and hold the desired phrase, and select "**Highlight**" from the pop-up menu.

To **Bookmark** the page where the search term appears, click on the Bookmark Icon, which appears at the upper right-hand portion of the screen, pictured below in **Figure 69**.

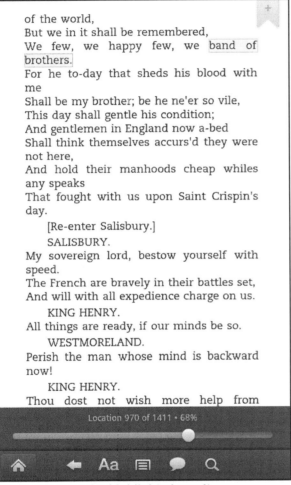

Figure 69: Note the highlighted result.

Once you've added a bookmark, you can find it by tapping the Menu button. You'll see the following screen pop up, which will show you all of your **Bookmarks**, **Comments** and **Highlights**.

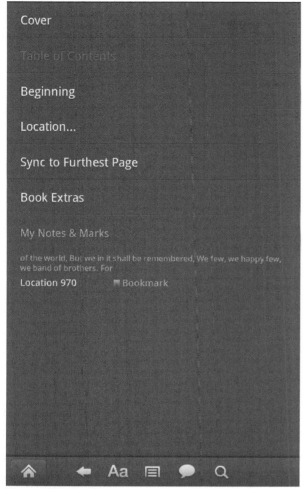

Figure 70: The Menu page. Note the Bookmark for 'Location 970' at the bottom.

In our example, above, when you tapped and held on "band of brothers", you probably saw a definition for the word that your finger was actually resting on. And that's our next topic, the digital dictionary. Your Kindle Fire enables you to have both your book and your dictionary in one package—pretty cool indeed.

TIP: Your Kindle automatically "remembers" the last page you were reading before exiting a book. So you don't need to enter a bookmark every time you quit reading an eBook; the correct page will appear the next time you open the book.

Using Kindle's New American Oxford Dictionary

Included as standard equipment with your Kindle Fire is a free copy of *The New Oxford American Dictionary*, which you can find in your **Books** library. The really neat thing is, you can access the entire dictionary while you're reading an eBook or other document. When you encounter an unfamiliar word, simply tap and hold it. A pop-up menu will appear with an abridged definition. To see the complete *New Oxford* entry, tap the menu item "**Full Definition.**"

You can also open the Kindle's dictionary by itself and scroll through the whole thing—just in case you run out of eBooks ;-)

By the way, do you enjoy listening to music while you're reading? Or just plain listening? Then you're going to love what's coming up next.

6 ► MUSIC TO YOUR EARS VIA KINDLE FIRE

We've talked about video, we've talked about print, and now we're talking about music. Yes, the Kindle Fire is a multimedia machine. When it comes to digital music, your options are wide open. You can buy it from Amazon and load it right on your device or stream it from the Cloud to save storage space on your device. You can load your existing music collection onto your Kindle Fire. And you can purchase more music through Apple's iTunes Store and other providers.

Your Kindle Fire plays MP3 files, the most common format for digital music. And the Fire has some great features to enhance your listening pleasure, like finding long-lost album artwork.

Loading music from your computer. Perhaps you've already accumulated some music you've downloaded to your computer or copied from CDs. You can easily move it to your Kindle Fire:

1. Plug in your Kindle Fire using the **Mini USB** connection
2. Open a **Windows Explorer** window to view your device
3. Navigate to the **Music** folder
4. Open another **Windows Explorer** window and navigate to the music directory on your computer, which will vary, depending upon where you store your music.

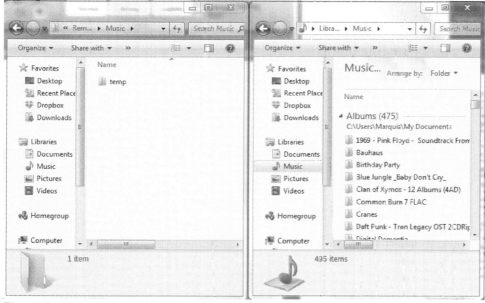

Figure 71: Open two Windows Explorer windows

To transfer music, simply drag and drop the folder you want to copy to your Kindle Fire. Upon completion, you'll see the files in the **Music** folder of your Kindle.

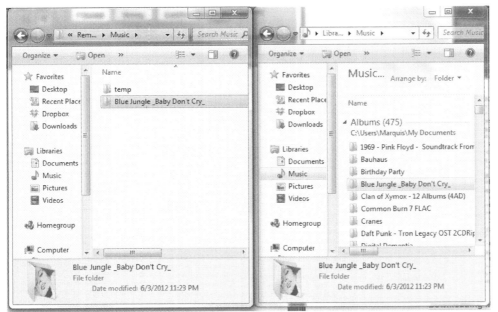

Figure 72: Transferring the album 'Baby Don't Cry' from My Computer to Kindle.

After you've made the transfer, navigate to the **Music Library** on your Kindle to see the results.

Figure 73: The album appears in my Kindle Music Library, complete with cover art.

If you have a massive music collection, you may want to consider storing it in the Cloud to conserve space on your device. We'll discuss this shortly.

Navigating the music library

Once again, we see that your **Library** is a lynchpin of your Kindle Fire. Navigate to your **home-screen** and then select Music from your top menu. You'll arrive at your **Music** library.

Along the top of your **Music** library, you'll see a row of selections. On the top, you'll see **Cloud** and **Device**. Below, you'll see **Playlists**, **Artists**, **Albums** and **Songs**. The familiar **Store >** link is also found along the top of the device, pictured below.

Figure 74: The Music Library top menu selections

As always, the items highlighted in orange denote your existing location in the library. In **Figure 74**, for instance, I'm viewing the music on my **Device** using the **Albums** view.

Several different views are available: **Playlists** shows lists of songs you've built from your music collection (more on this later). **Artists** sorts your music by artist name. **Albums** sorts your collection by album format, and **Songs** lists individual songs you have stored on your device on in the Cloud, depending upon the view you've selected.

Searching for Music

If you can't easily find a song that you have in your collection, click on the **Magnifying Glass** at the bottom of the **Music** library screen to open up the **Search** option.

Uploading audio files to Cloud

Amazon's Cloud provides an alternate means of storing your music. The basic plan gives you 5GB of storage for your music collection, and you can upgrade to an unlimited storage plan if necessary.

To upload music to the Cloud, you'll need to download the "Amazon MP3 Uploader," a free application that locates music files on your computer and copies them to the Cloud. The uploader is compatible with MP3 files and ACC files, which you may have if you're an iTunes user.

Visit http://www.amazon.com/cloudplayer to access the music you have stored on the Amazon Cloud. If you haven't uploaded any yet, you'll see the following screen.

amazon cloud player
Hello, Marquis Dufek. | Settings | Sign Out | Help | amazon MP3 store
Upload your music
Your Cloud Drive Music
Songs
Albums
Artists
Genres
Deleted Items
Playlists
Latest Purchases
Latest Uploads
+ Create New Playlist
Your Cloud Drive Music > Songs
You have no music stored in your Amazon Cloud Drive
You have 5.0 GB of free Cloud Drive storage remaining.
Upload your music
or
Shop for music in the Amazon MP3 Store
Cloud Player for Android
View larger
No songs playing.

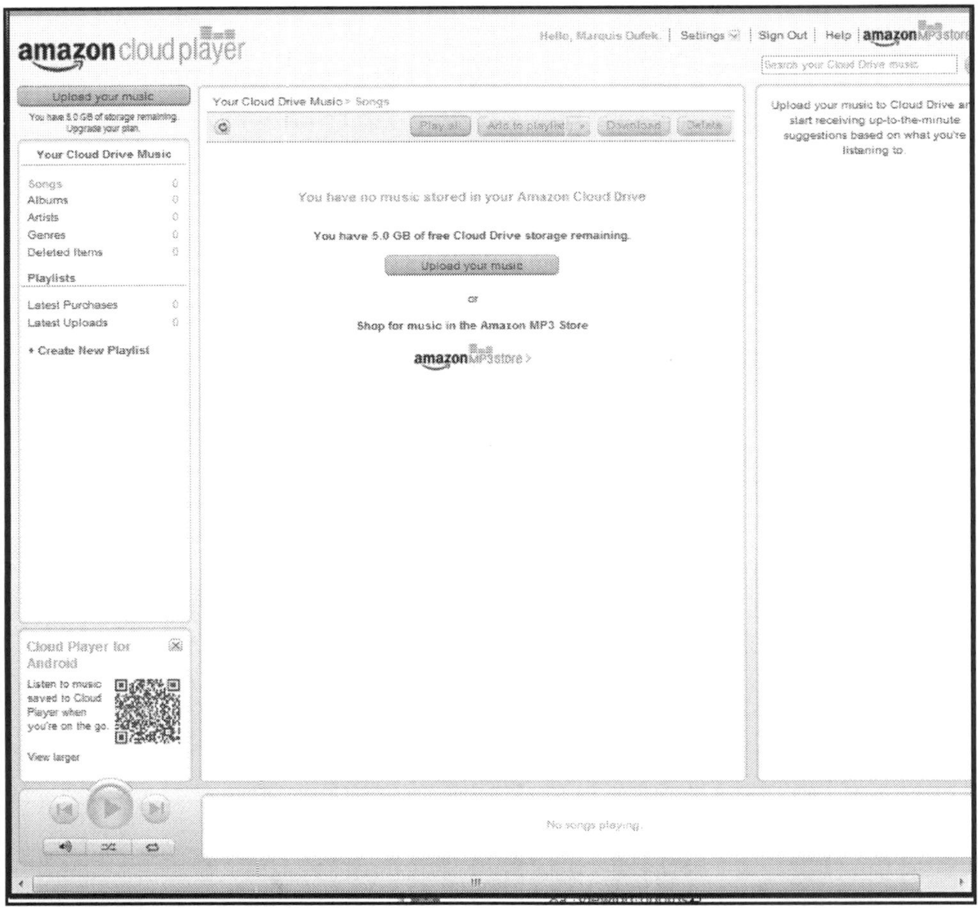

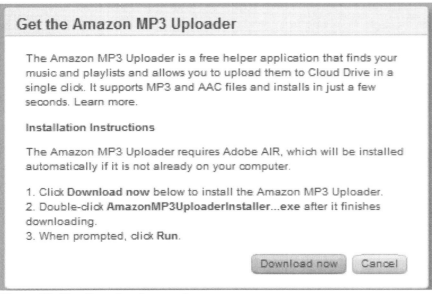

Figure 75: The MP3 Uploader home-page.

Click on "**Upload your music.**" If you already have the MP3 Uploader installed, you'll be taken to the application. If not, you'll see the screen pictured in **Figure 76**.

Get the Amazon MP3 Uploader
The Amazon MP3 Uploader is a free helper application that finds your music and playlists and allows you to upload them to Cloud Drive in a single click. It supports MP3 and AAC files and installs in just a few seconds. Learn more.
Installation Instructions
The Amazon MP3 Uploader requires Adobe AIR, which will be installed automatically if it is not already on your computer.
1. Click Download now below to install the Amazon MP3 Uploader.
2. Double-click AmazonMP3UploaderInstaller...exe after it finishes downloading.
3. When prompted, click Run.
Download now
Cancel

Figure 76: The Download prompt.

Install the application and it will begin searching your computer for audio files. If you want to handle the search manually, click the option on the prompt and you'll be presented with the option to browse manually, pictured in **Figure 77**, below.

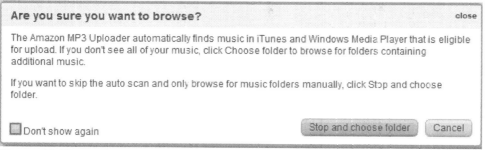

Figure 77: The option to browse manually.

TIP: If you have a very large music collection and don't want to wait for the entire collection to upload, transfer the albums you want to upload to a separate directory on your computer. Then you can browse that directory manually.

If you want to manually browse, choose "**Stop and choose folder**" as shown in **Figure 77**.
After you choose the option to browse manually, you'll be able to select a folder from your system tree. Highlight the folder you want, and the MP3 uploader will scan it for files that are eligible for cloud storage, shown in **Figures 78** and **79**.

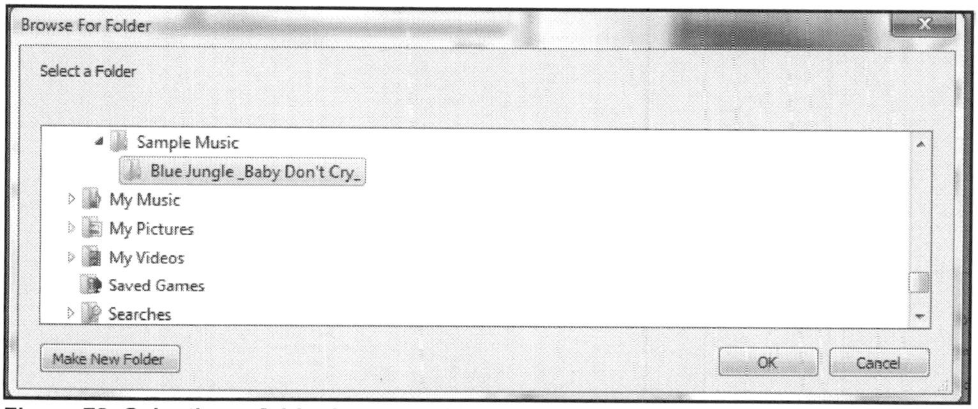

Figure 78: Selecting a folder by manual browsing.

Figure 79: The MP3 Uploader detects eligible uploads.

The uploading process can take considerable time, even with a speedy Internet connection. After completion, you can see your albums on the Amazon Cloud page and, by selecting "**Cloud**" in your Music library, you can view the files from your Kindle Fire, too.

Remember: You need a Wi-Fi connection to play music stored in the Cloud.

Playing songs

Playing songs on your Kindle Fire couldn't be easier. There is a built-in application that will handle it for you, but you can also download apps that give you different options for playing music (we'll review some in Chapter 9). For now, let's explore the Kindle Fire's built-in music player.

To play a song, open up album you want to listen to by tapping on it in your **Music** library. This will give you a list of tracks.

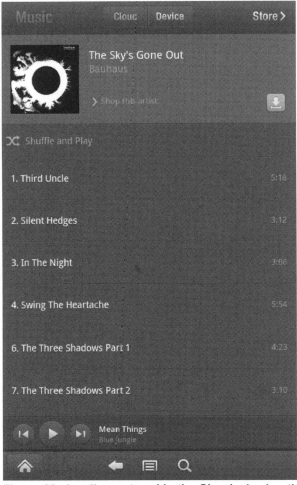

Figure 80: An album stored in the Cloud, viewing the track listing.

Review the interface in Figure 80. The "> **Shop this artist**" link will auto-search Amazon for more material from the current artist. The orange downward-pointing arrow to the right of "**Shop this artist**" will download the album from the Cloud to your device's internal storage.

The **Shuffle and Play** button allows you to switch between playing the album's tracks in the original sequence or randomly.

Below the track listing, you can see the controls for the player itself. They are, from right to left, go back one track, play/pause, advance one track.

As usual, you can click on the **Store >** icon to visit the Amazon music store and see what's available.

Internal and External Speakers

Kindle Fire is equipped with internal speakers suitable for listening to audio if the ambient noise is low. For better sound quality, you'll need to use headphones or external speakers.

Your Kindle Fire has a 1/8" auxiliary output jack right next to the power button. This type of connection is fairly common among different manufacturers' headphones, earbuds, and computer speakers. Also, adapters are available to help match the connections of various equipment.

Sound quality

Your Kindle Fire should provide very high quality sound. If you're experiencing difficulty using external speakers, here are some troubleshooting tips:

Sound not audible: Check the volume level on the Kindle and the volume level on the external speakers. If this does not resolve the problem, make sure that all jacks are firmly in their slots and that the speakers are plugged in to a wall socket, if applicable.

"Fuzzy" or distorted audio: Turn down the volume level on your Kindle Fire and turn up the level on your speakers to compensate. Having too high a volume level on your Kindle Fire combined with too low a volume on the speakers or headphones can cause distortion.

Thin or weak sound: Check the bitrate of your MP3. Most of them will be between 128 and 256 kbps. If the bitrate is too low, it may be the MP3 that's the problem.

Mono sound: Check your connections. A plug may not be fully inserted.

TIP: Be careful when using headphones. Because they go directly in or over your ear canal, they can cause permanent hearing loss at high volume. If you cannot hear ambient sounds—or your ears ring after listening to music on your Kindle Fire—turn down the volume.

Creating playlists

Playlists allow you to create what amounts to a mix CD on the fly. You can combine any song you own into a playlist that will play in sequential mode or shuffle, depending upon which method you select. The process is very easy and you can use music stored in the Cloud or on your device.

Creating your List

1. Open your **Music** library
2. Click on **Playlists** at the top of the menu
3. Select "**Create new playlist**"
4. Type in a name
5. Click the **Plus** sign next to a song to add it to the list. See **Figure 81**.

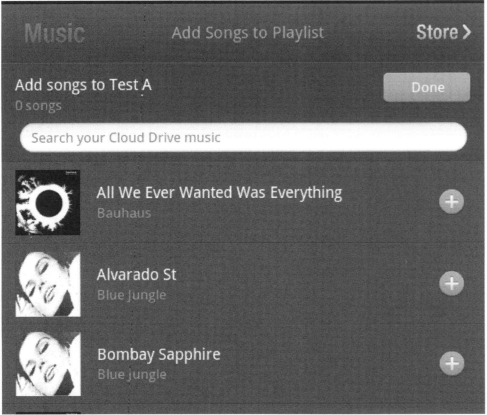

Figure 81

6. The song name will go gray once you select it
7. Tap "**Done**" when you're finished

Editing the list

1. Open your **Music** library
2. Select the playlist that you want to change from the list that appears below the "**Create a new playlist**" button. If it doesn't show up, click on "**Playlists**" on top to get a complete list
3. Select "**Edit**" at the top of the screen to edit the list. See **Figure 82**.

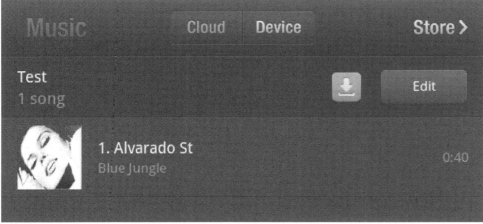

Figure 82

4. Remove a track by clicking the **Minus** sign

5. To change the order in which the song plays, tap and hold the song and drag it to the desired position

6. To add a track, click the "**Add**" button next to the "**Save**" button

7. To save the list, click "**Save**"

The **Playlist** feature allows you to create mixes for any occasion. Make one for parties, for relaxing at home or for long drives. The Kindle Fire makes it easy to organize and enjoy your music collection!

Remember: If you're making a playlist for a trip, be sure to download it from the cloud by clicking on the orange **Download** button: the downward-pointing arrow pictured in **Figure 82**.

7 ▶ VIDEO ON THE KINDLE FIRE

The Kindle Fire is a versatile video player. Along with its great picture quality, the Fire provides access to Amazon's vast library of downloadable and streaming content.

In Chapter 3 we reviewed how to browse and buy video. Once you've purchased a video, it will appear in your video library or, if you choose to watch it from the Amazon servers, it will begin streaming immediately.

When you choose to purchase an Amazon Prime eligible movie, you'll be presented with the option to stream it or buy it, along with additional purchase options.

Figure 83: The Video download page

Select "**More Purchase Options**" and you'll get the following pop-up, pictured in **Figure 84**.

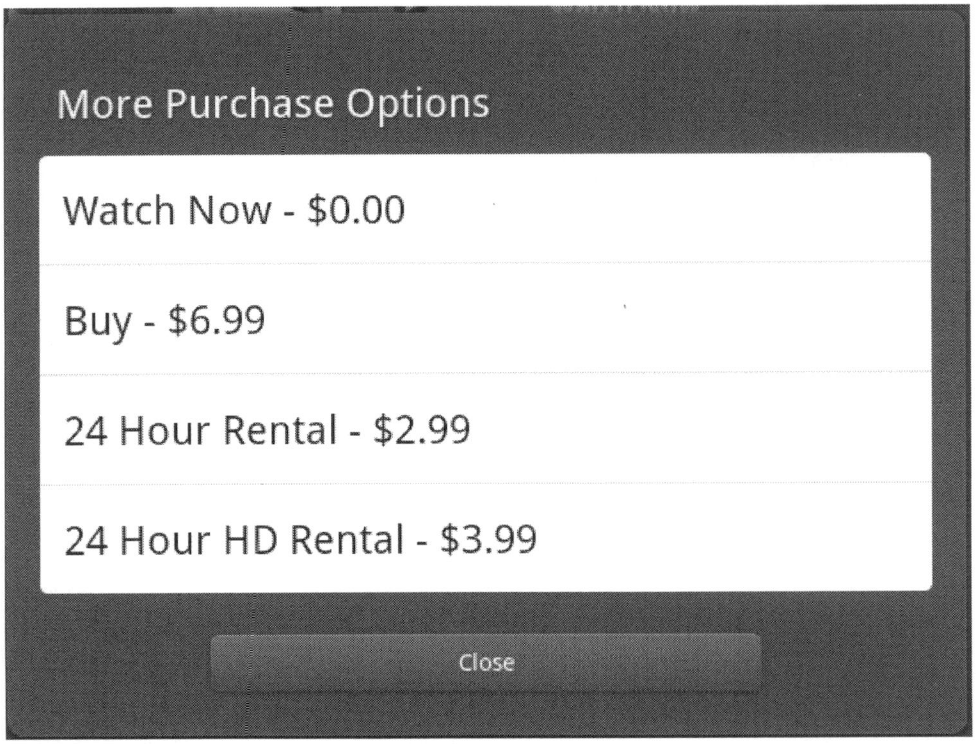

Figure 84: Additional Video Purchase Options

If you choose any of the purchase options other than "**Watch Now**," (streaming) the Video will appear in your Video library.

TIP: Because of the large file sizes, it's usually preferable to leave video content in the Cloud to preserve space on your device. You might make an exceptions in certain cases—perhaps you'd want to store a couple of movies while you're on vacation away from your home network. Remember, your device has about 5 GB of internal storage, and video files can approach 1 GB each.

If you choose one of the **24 Hour Rental** options, the video will be returned automatically for you. And just like Kindle library books, you don't have to worry about late fees when you rent a video.

Controlling Videos

Your Kindle Fire has a built-in video player with simple, intuitive controls. See **Figure 85** below to view the video player interface.

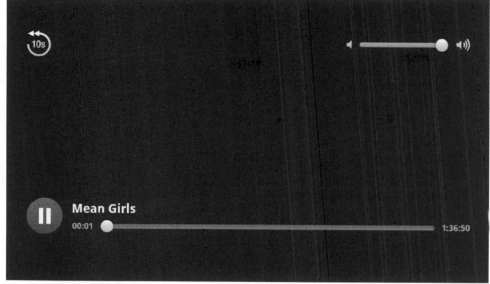

Figure 85: The Kindle Fire video player

In the illustration above, you can see the **Play/Pause** button on the far left. Tap the button to begin viewing the video. The illustration shows the **Pause** button, denoted by the || sign.

The slider—shown at 00:01 in the movie—allows you to use your finger to skip forward or reverse in the video. If play is interrupted, your video will automatically resume at the point where playback stopped.

The Volume slider is at the top right corner of the screen, set to maximum volume in the illustration above. The upper left corner of the screen is the buffer indicator. The buffering process loads a bit of video into your player so that if your Internet connection slows momentarily, playback will continue normally. When the buffering cycle has completed, the indicator disappears.

TIP: If you have choppy, stuttering playback, be sure to check your Internet connection. You might also want to try shutting down apps that may be running in the background and slowing performance. As a last resort, try rebooting.

Streaming video versus downloading video

"Streamed" video is simply video which is stored remotely, and not on your personal device or Cloud account. If you've ever watched YouTube or accessed the Netflix online service, you're familiar with streaming, which is highly dependent on your Internet connection.

By contrast, "local" video files are stored directly on your device. You can download them via Wi-Fi or load them from your computer via **Mini USB**. Once stored on your device, they can be accessed without an Internet connection.

Streaming and local video have advantages and disadvantages:

Streaming Pros

- No local storage space required.
- No downloading time required.
- Wide availability.
- You can easily abandon the video and you don't have to delete the file.

- Streaming services offer good selection and economy through Amazon Prime or outside services such as Netflix.

Streaming Cons
- Continuous Wi-Fi connection is required.
- Playback may be interrupted by network issues.
- Video may not be available after a time.
- Selection is more limited compared to downloaded options.

Local Pros
- Stutter-free playback.
- Fast loading, no delays or buffering.
- Video quality may be superior to streaming services.
- You own the video and can archive it on your computer

Local Cons
- Consumes lots of storage space.
- Requires outright purchase, can be more expensive.
- If you lose your devices with local storage, you've permanently lost the content.
- Self-loaded videos—transferred from your computer— do not appear in your Kindle Fire's **Video** library.

Streaming from YouTube and other sites

Using your Kindle Fire, you can play Flash videos, a format that's widely used online. You have to turn on Flash from your **Browser Settings** menu.

1. Open your browser
2. Tap the **Menu** icon
3. Tap "**Settings**"

Flash videos and content in other supported Internet formats cannot be accessed via the **Video** library; you must view them using the Silk web browser.

Navigating the Video Library

The **Video Library** section of your Kindle is accessed from the top of the screen menu on your **home-screen**. This brings you to a listing of all your videos. By default, however, you'll arrive at Amazon's video store, including those that may be downloaded or streamed. To navigate from Amazon's video store to your personal video collection, select the "**Library >**" link at the top right corner of the screen.

The menu items should look familiar. The main difference is that you'll see **Movie** and **TV** atop the screen. Content you've purchased from Amazon will be sorted into its proper categories.

Figure 86: The Video Library interface.

To select any video from your library, simply tap on the icon. To get the extended list of option, tap and hold the icon.

To delete any video that you've downloaded, go to the product detail page for that video by tapping on its icon. Select "**Delete**" from the download box. You'll get a confirmation and the video will be deleted after you confirm that selection.

Where are my home videos?

While you can load videos onto your Amazon Kindle Fire with your **Mini USB**, they won't appear in your **Video library.** But in the next section, we'll explore the Kindle Fire's gallery features, which will enable you to navigate to these videos.

8 ▶ VIEWING HOME VIDEO AND PHOTOS

Personal photos and videos that you load onto your Kindle Fire are handled differently than media you buy from Amazon. While your Amazon video content goes straight to your Video Library, your personal videos are accessed from the **Gallery** application.

Transferring photos to Kindle

Transferring photos from your computer to your Kindle Fire is easy:

1. Connect your Kindle Fire to your computer using a **Mini USB.**
2. Browse to the "**Pictures**" folder on your Kindle Fire.
3. Open up another File Browser (Windows Explorer on Windows) window on your computer and browse to the directory of photos you want.
4. Drag and drop the photos from your computer to your Kindle Fire photos directory.

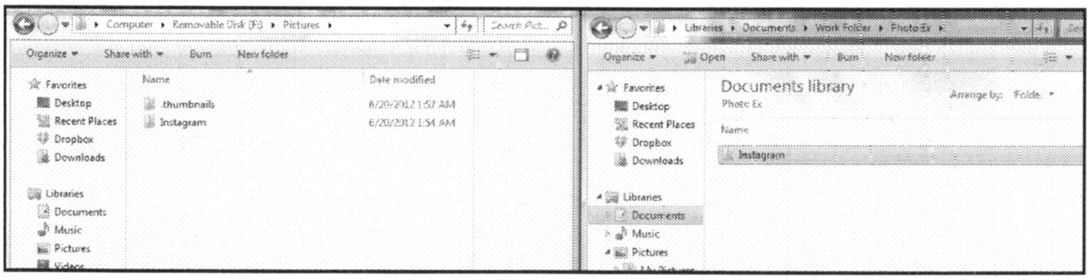

Figure 87: The Kindle Fire directory is on the left, the folder being copied is on the right.

Viewing photos

Photos are viewed using the **Gallery** app, which you'll find preloaded in your **Apps** library. Just tap it to open your photos. The app will access photos and video from their respective folders, along with thumbnails for any album art you uploaded with your music.

Figure 88: The Gallery app is depicted by the filmstrip graphic. Tap it to open.

The **Gallery** app has a great interface that lets you see all of your images and videos. If you have more than can be accommodated on one screen, you can tap and drag to move the file listings. When you open the app, you'll see the screen pictured in **Figure 89**.

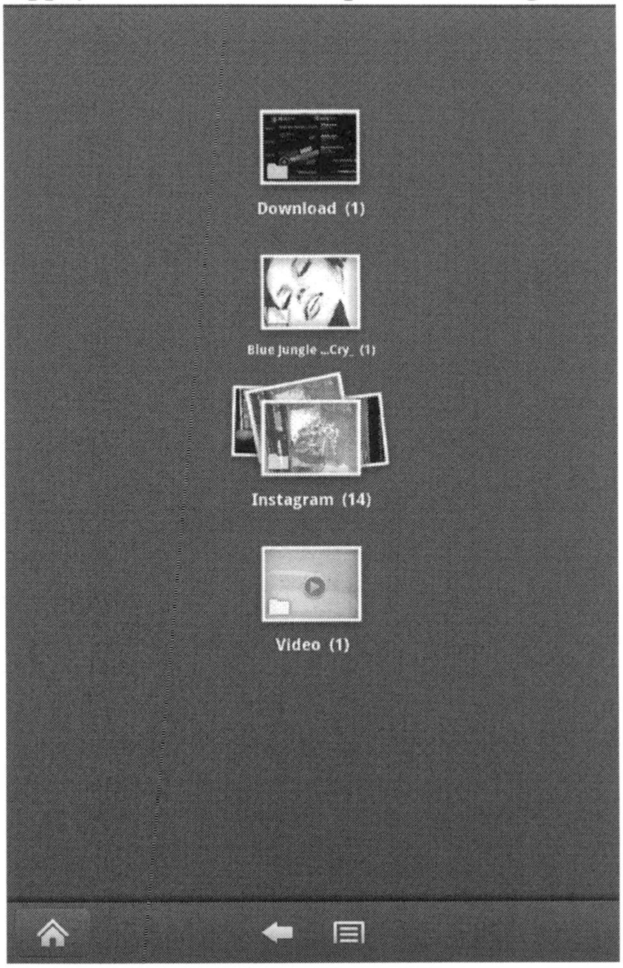

Figure 89: The Gallery App Opened Up

The buttons on the **Gallery** app work as you'll remember them from other Kindle Fire screens. The **Menu** button will give you the option to share your images via social-networking sites, to delete a folder, or to get additional information on any of the folders.

Tap on any folder to see a thumbnail listing of its contents.

Figure 90: The photo thumbnails for the Instagram folder pictured in Figure 88.

The thumbnails provide an easy way to navigate the content of any of your folders. You can spin them around, scroll them up and down and move them around in a lot of other ways. The interface, in this regard, is fun to use. To open a photo, tap on its thumbnail.

Viewing photos, working with tools

When you open up a photo, it will display at a size appropriate for your screen orientation. Most photos are best viewed in landscape orientation because they appear larger.

When you open a photo, you'll see three icons beneath it, pictured in **Figure 91**.

Figure 91: The photo tools

The right-most icon on the top of the image, which resembles three stacked rectangles, starts a **Slideshow**. It will continue through all of the images in the folder you're viewing. Tap it again to stop the slideshow. The **Magnifying Glasses** zoom out or in to the photo, respectively.

The **Menu** button at the bottom gives you access to share, delete and info options.

You can zoom into photos with finger gestures, in much the same way that you can adjust the view of web pages.

Figure 92: A photo displayed in Kindle Fire's photo viewer.

TIP: Amazon Cloud storage is an economical method for backing up priceless family photos and other important documents. Once there, you can access the files from any device with Internet connectivity.

Transferring home videos and viewing on Kindle

Home videos, as mentioned previously, are handled differently than the video content you purchase from Amazon. They don't appear in your Fire's **Video** library; you instead access them from your **Gallery** app. The files are shown as thumbnails with a right-pointing arrow superimposed upon them, pictured below in **Figure 93**.

Figure 93: A video thumbnail in the Gallery app.

Tap the **Video thumbnail** to launch the video player. The Kindle Fire supports the MP4 and VP8 video formats. These formats are available on most camcorders and cellular phones. In the event that your existing videos aren't Kindle-compatible, there are applications for converting the format. One such application for PCs, **Any Video Converter Free Edition**, can be downloaded here: http://www.pcworld.com/downloads/file/fid,74199-order,4/description.html.

9 ▶ APPS FOR KINDLE FIRE

With the potential to download apps created by thousands of Android developers, your Kindle Fire's horizons are virtually unlimited. We've explored the App library previously, and now it's time to actually look at some of the apps that take the Kindle Fire to another level beyond its out-of-the-box functionality.

Although you can obtain apps from many sources, the most convenient and safe option is dealing directly with Amazon's own App Store. You can access from your device, or from your computer at www.amazon.com/b?node=2350149011.

Figure 94: The XiiaLive Lite Interface.

TIP: Never download an app from an unknown source. Untrusted apps can cause technical difficulty and pose a security risk.

Apps for Fun

Plenty of great apps can be loaded onto your Kindle Fire that provide different types of entertainment and to customize the look and feel of your device.

XiiaLive Lite

No matter how much great music you have stored on your device or available in the Cloud, occasionally you'd rather hear something fresh and new. Streaming Internet music provides relief. For example, Internet radio stations broadcast online, offering an incredible variety of music in every genre. If you want someone else do the work of selecting the tunes, streaming radio is a great option and that brings us to our first app: XiiaLive Lite. The Lite version is free; a paid upgrade offers more features and no advertising.

XiiaLive Lite allows you to play Internet streams in most formats, and you can open them directly from your browser when you find the web page they're hosted on.

To find and download this app, search the App Store for "XiiaLive."

TIP: Check the webpages of your local broadcast radio stations to see if they have a stream also.

Go Launcher EX

The Kindle Fire interface is, to put it bluntly, a bit plain. But you can customize the look to suit exactly how you use it. Enter Go Launcher EX.

You can't download Go Launcher EX from the Amazon App Store because Amazon hasn't approved the app. Go Launcher allows you to customize your interface however you want and, because of that, you can set up your Kindle to be an even better productivity and entertainment tool. All of your Amazon libraries and other functions will still be there; but they appear as an application rather than as the default layout for your screen. Even though you might prefer to use your Fire this way, Amazon would prefer that you're constantly bombarded with offers to purchase new content.

Go Launcher's homepage is http://golauncher.goforandroid.com/.

To illustrate how radically you can change Kindle Fire's interface, see the figure below. The Go Launcher EX app has a huge number of themes that you can apply. In **Figure 95**, you can see that I've added weather, XiiaLive and the Amazon default desktop—shown as "**Launcher**"—to my desktop for easy access.

Figure 95: Kindle Fire interface altered with Go Launcher EX.

TIP: Altering the Kindle Fire interface may make things a bit confusing for you at first. It's best to master all of the default settings from the Amazon interface and then to expand your options as far as looks go, if you prefer.

The interface on Go Launcher EX is designed for any Android device, so it includes icons related to cellular phones, which you can remove.

Angry Birds

You've surely heard the name. Angry Birds is a game that allows you to enjoy some classic, addicting arcade-style gaming on your Kindle Fire. It's free, and you can download it instantly from the Amazon App Store. Kids of all ages enjoy this one, and it can make long road trips more tolerable.

TIP: Many apps, Angry Birds included, have a free version that contains advertising, and a paid version without ads. If you really love the free version, it's hard to resist buying the paid version for a few dollars more. But this free/paid system enables you to sample almost everything without risking a dime.

Utilities

Some of the utilities available for the Kindle Fire keep you safe and make it easier to get the most out of it. Here are a few to consider.

Kaspersky Tablet Security

Not too many years ago, people using the Macintosh operating system enjoyed bragging that they were free of viruses and malware. Nowadays, this type of scourge is affecting Mac users, too, and Android isn't immune either.

Kaspersky has consistently gotten good reviews for its antivirus products for mobile devices. You'll have to download it from their website, however.

TIP: There are free anti-virus applications on the Amazon App Store and on other sites, so it pays to shop around.

Wi-Fi Analyzer Free

The Kindle Fire needs a Wi-Fi to connect to the Internet and, sometimes, you need a bit more information than the Settings panel gives you. This is where Wi-Fi Analyzer Free really shines. It gives you a great deal of information on the wireless networks around you, including a meter that shows you their strength. This makes it a lot easier to find the sweet spots in some buildings where the Wi-Fi might work better than in others. It also allows you to see how many networks are in your area and whether or not yours may be on a channel that is too crowded.

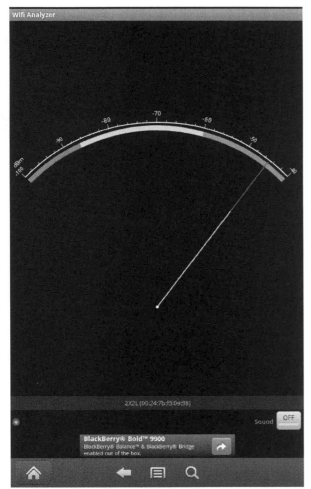

Figure 96: The Wi-Fi Analyzer Free's nifty analog meter interface.

imo

The **imo** app allows you to connect to multiple types of instant-messaging services. You won't have voice chat on it, but you can certainly text chat all you want, making it a great choice for anyone who uses these services for work or pleasure.

The imo app is compatible with:

- AIM
- Facebook Chat
- Google Talk
- ICQ
- Jabber
- MSN
- MySpace Chat
- Skype
- Yahoo

Sometimes, the best thing about a Kindle Fire is that it lets you get away from your desktop computer and still enjoy everything the Internet has to offer. With imo, you can be sure that you don't miss any important messages when you get away from your desk for a while!

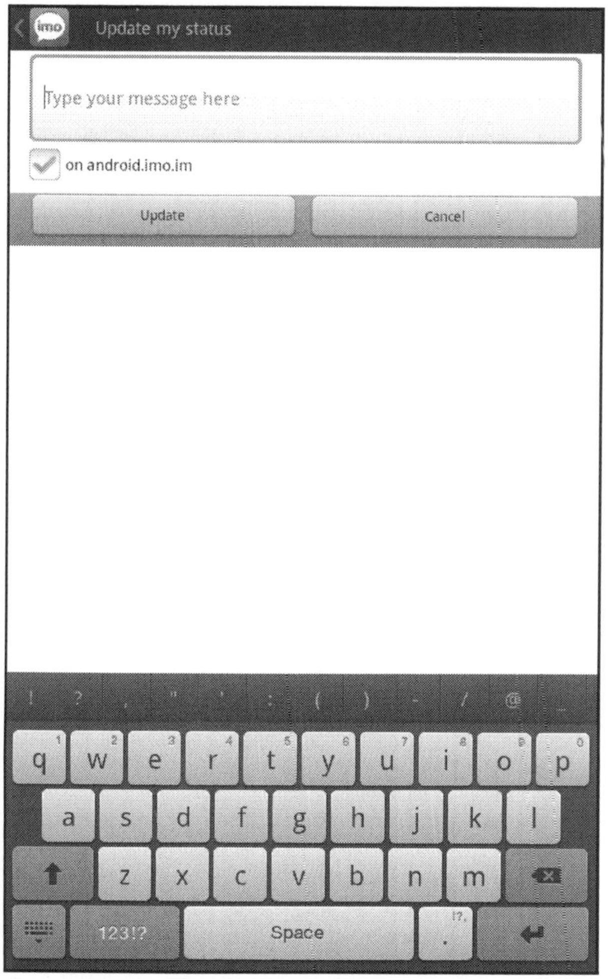

Figure 97: Let your friends know you're on your Kindle Fire!

Productivity

QuickOffice

QuickOffice allows you to open and edit documents in the most popular office formats, including Microsoft. It's a required equipment if you plan on using your Kindle Fire as a productivity tool. Fortunately, it's right in your **App** library by default.

To use QuickOffice, tap its icon and accept the license agreement. If you want the pro version of this software, you can purchase it from the Amazon App Store. It's one of the handiest utilities to have on your Kindle Fire.

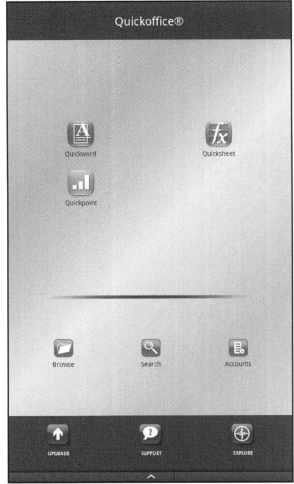

Figure 98: The QuickOffice welcome screen.

Evernote

Evernote is an application that allows you to write notes, take picture notes, record audio notes, clip web pages, and much more. If you do research in any capacity—for fun or business—it's a must. You can share your notes between your devices, so whatever you clip on your PC or Mac will be available on your Kindle Fire.

Figure 99: The Evernote icon

Office Calculator Free

The Office Calculator Free program is a great choice for anyone who wants more advanced capabilities out of their calculator but doesn't venture into trigonometry or other advanced forms of math. As the name says, if you need an office calculator, this one might be for you. It even keeps a tape of your calculations! The free version has small advertisements at the top of the screen, pictured in Figure 100. The paid version does not.

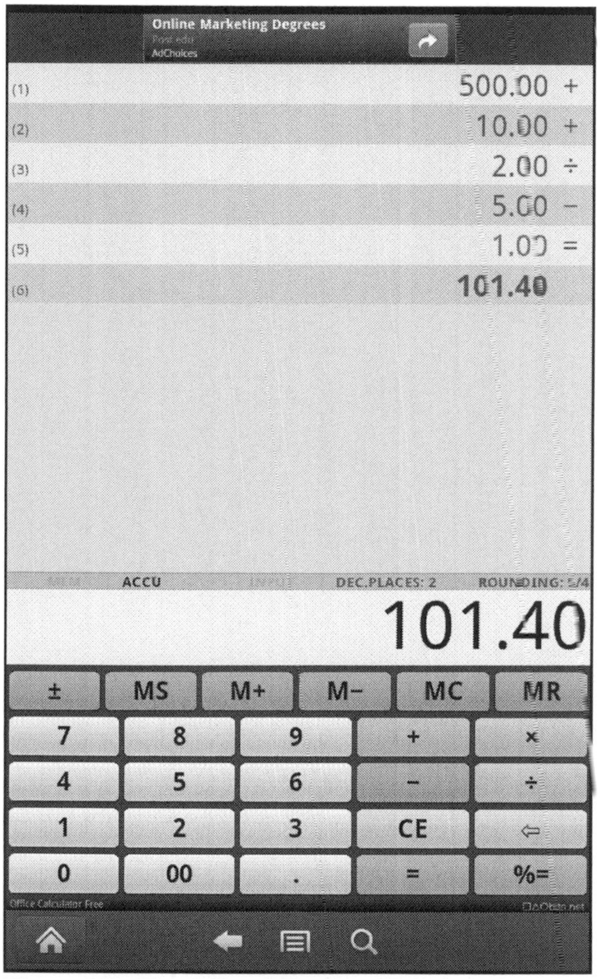

Figure 100: The Office Calculator Free interface.

Managing apps

Apps consume storage space on your device. So if you install an app and you don't like it, remember to uninstall it to free up that space. You don't want your Kindle stuffed with apps you don't want. The instructions for uninstalling apps can be found in Chapter 3.

To check your App storage quickly:
1. Click on the **Gear Icon**
2. Tap **Device**
3. Look for "**Application Storage**".

TIP: The ratings on apps in the Amazon App Store are a good indication of their quality. Be sure to scan the reviews before investing time or money with an app.

Free your Kindle

If you want to install apps from locations other than the Amazon App Store, you'll have to select the appropriate option on your Kindle:

1. Tap your **Gear Icon**
2. Tap "**More**"
3. Tap "**Device**"
4. Set "**Allow Installation of Applications From Unknown Sources**" to "**On**"

This allows you to install applications from any source that you wish. Remember, however, that applications from sources other than Amazon might not be tested or safe.

TIP: The Google Play Store is the largest marketplace for Android apps. Your Kindle Fire works on the Android operating system but installing apps from Google Play is about as convenient as trying to get water to run uphill. There are other sites you can explore that make it easier. They include:

- Only Android, www.onlyandroid.mobihand.com/
- GetJar, www.getjar.com/.
- SlideMe, www.slideme.org/.

10 ▶ FEED YOUR KINDLE WITH WEB CONTENT

After all that discussion about apps, videos, pictures and web browsing, it might be easy to forget that the Kindle Fire is, first and foremost, an eReader. Not all eReaders can handle the same formats and Kindle devices are no exception.

Amazon benefits mightily from consumer loyalty. By linking their device so strongly to the AZW and MOBI formats they use, they make the average user assume they can only read eBooks that are bought directly from Amazon. Fortunately, you actually can read any eBook format you want, thanks to a great program called Calibre, a program that runs on Windows or Mac desktop computers. Calibre is free, it's stable and, to put it in the most direct terms, it's awesome—it can deliver you hundreds of dollars' worth of newspaper, magazine and book content every day, 365 days a year. The only challenge is finding the time to read that gusher of great content you're piping to your Kindle.

Using Calibre with the Kindle Fire EBook Reader

Let's jump right in and download the Calibre application right now. I have been using the program, along with thousands of others, for the past three years. The best things in life are free, and believe me, Calibre is one of them.

- Go to http://calibre-ebook.com/ and select "Download Calibre"
- Open the downloaded program to install the package once it's completed

On your first run, you'll get the **Welcome Wizard**. This is designed to help you set up your libraries and to import your books, as well as to help you select the correct device!

The first screen, pictured in **Figure 101** will set your **Calibre Library** directory. The default choice is a good one.

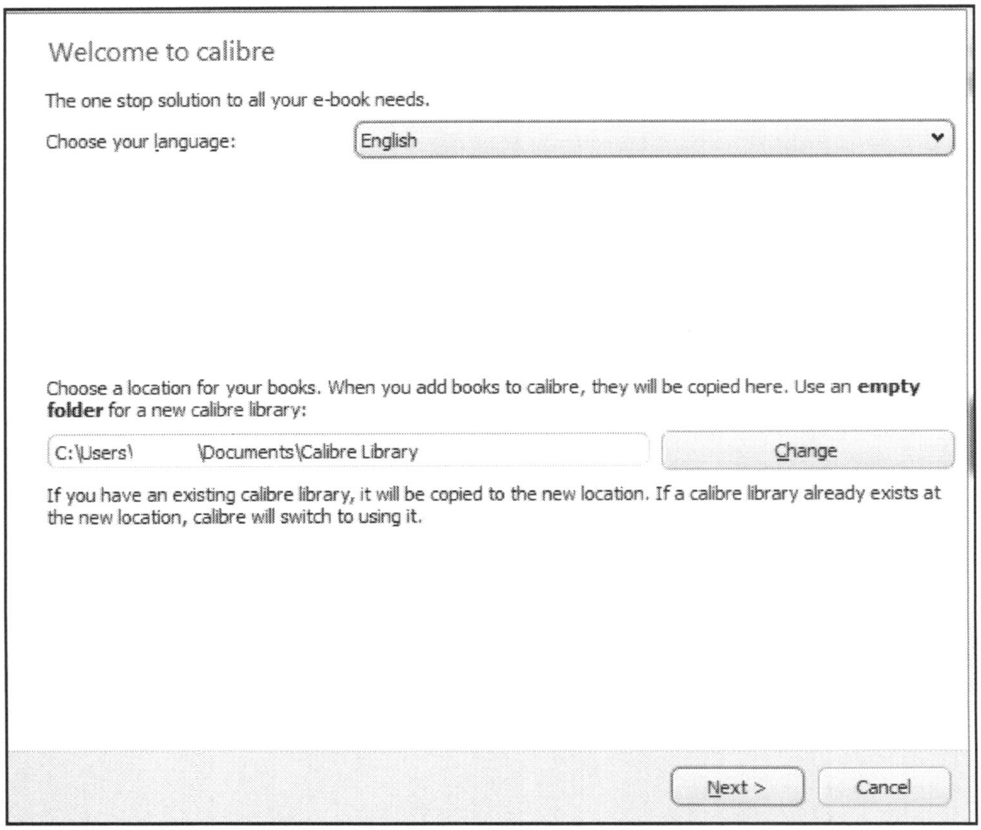

Figure 101: The Calibre Welcome Wizard screen 1

On the next screen, you'll have to choose your device. Obviously, choose Kindle Fire!

This sets the program up so that it knows to look for your Kindle Fire when you click the **Send to Device** icon.

When you have the program installed, launch it, and you'll see the screen shown in **Figure 103**. If you can't see all the icons across the top of the interface, simply expand the window until they fit.

Study the interface for a moment. This program is capable of doing many things; even offering you a way to shop for content across a number of different stores. What we'll concern ourselves with first, however, is opening up new sources of literature by using the features built into this program that allow you to convert books from other formats into ones that your Amazon Kindle can read.

All the news you can eat, and Calibre picks up the check

OK, I'll admit it. I'm a book nut. But I have an even bigger problem. I'm addicted to newspapers, too. I was a "news junkie" before anyone ever heard of such a thing. Twenty-five years ago, I paid about $75 a month to have three different newspapers dropped at my doorstep every morning—my local paper, The Wall Street Journal, and the New York Times. Now, since I discovered Calibre, I've been reading six newspapers a day—plus bunch of blogs and magazines like Newsweek and Time—and it doesn't cost me one red cent. The New York Times. The Washington Post. The New York Post. And, if I still have time, I can read The Onion and a couple others—just to get my humor fix. Your local newspaper is probably available, too. Calibre downloads the content they post on their websites, and sends it, nicely formatted, to your Kindle. The only cost is the few minutes you'll spend setting it up once, and then it works every day. Here how to get started:

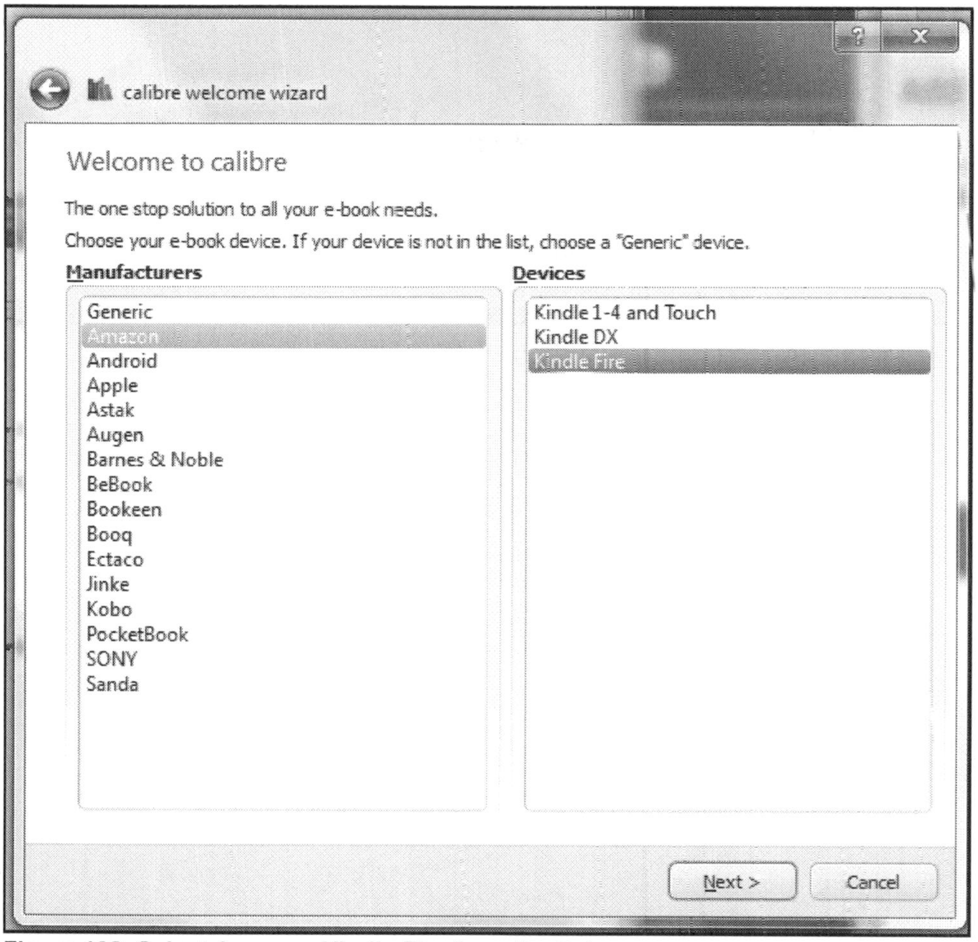

Figure 102: Select Amazon, Kindle Fire from the list.

1. Click on "**Fetch News**" in the Menu.
2. Select your language.
3. Select a news source.

In **Figure 115**, you can see that I've selected The Washington Post.

Note that I've opted to have it download automatically every day of the week after 6am. If you were the ultimate news junkie, you could set it to download the Associated Press news wire every 10 minutes. Calibre has hundreds of different news sources available in a huge number of languages, you just click them and enjoy—free.

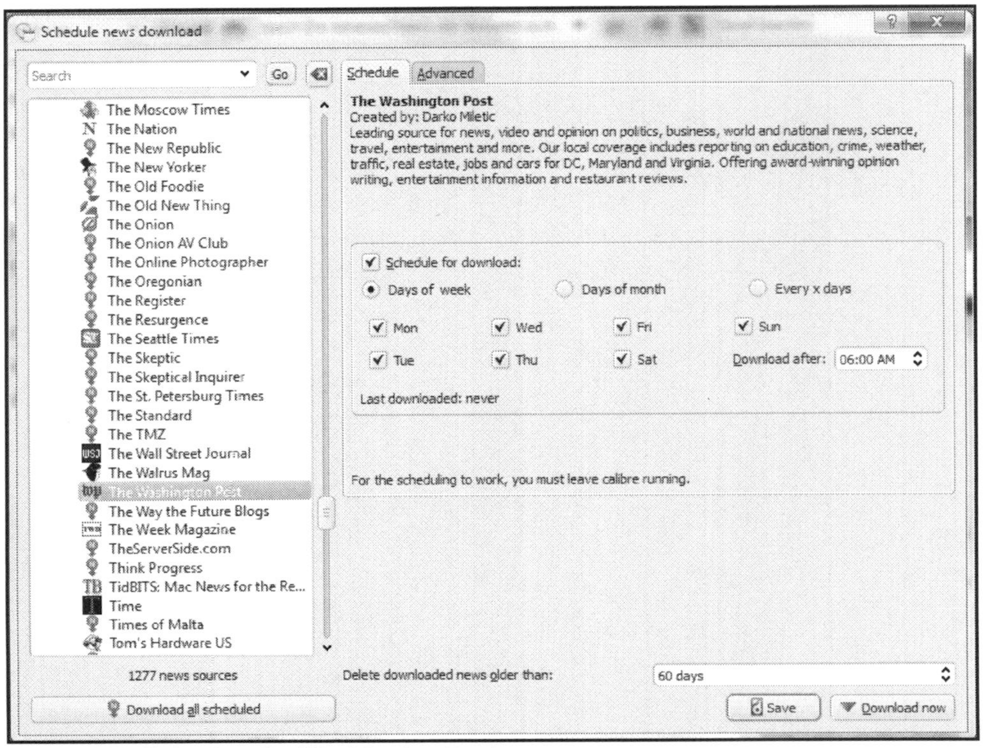

Figure 103: Selecting the Washington Post.

Of course, you have to leave Calibre running so it automatically downloads your news sources. If you have several news sites on your list, it will take a while. Personally, I leave my computer on 24/7, and Calibre is finding news for me constantly, and feeding my Kindle. In the old days, I used to finish my three newspapers and still want more. Now, with Calibre, I don't have a prayer of skimming everything I'm tempted to read every day.

TIP: In this section, we're talking about downloading content for free. It sounds too good to be true, but it's totally above board. We're not stealing, we're just using the stuff that publishers are posting to their websites. Calibre simply does the work of formatting it for the Kindle and email it to us.

After the news site has converted, you'll be able to transfer it to your Kindle Fire using the same interface that you use to transfer books. One of the best things about the Calibre program is that it's smart in meaningful ways. The program, for instance, will transfer newspapers to your Newsstand.

Figure 104: The Newsstand after transferring the converted news site.

Opening up the converted newspaper will give you a listing of all the articles it contains, separated by sections.

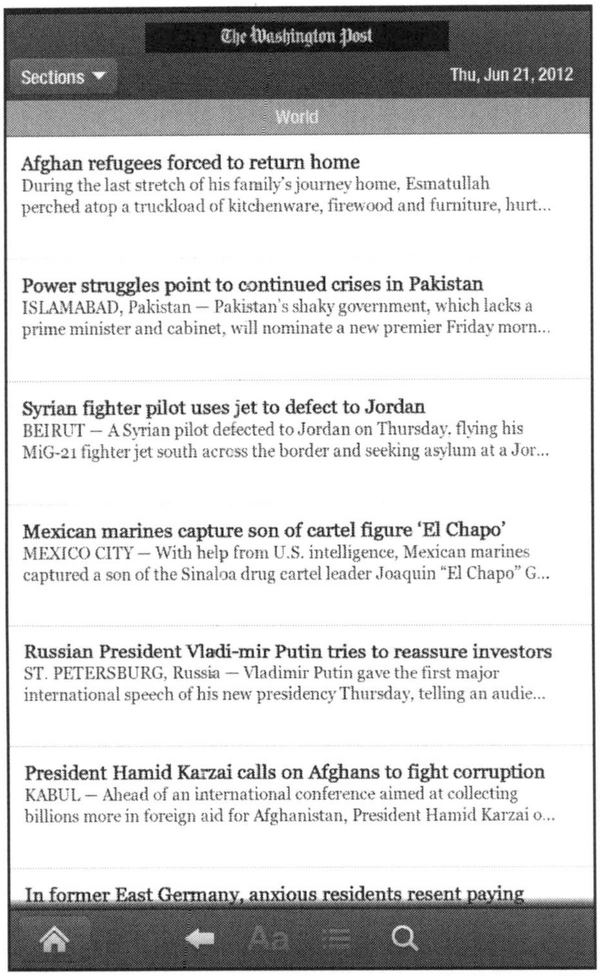

Figure 105: The converted newspaper's Table of Contents.

Tap any article to open it up and you'll be presented with the full text of the articles, and perhaps the photos, depending on the publication. Even better, the article opens up in the same comfortable format as the **Reading View** option in your browser for websites, which you can see in **Figure 118**, below.

So, is there any real difference between reading a newspaper website in reading view in your browser and reading it converted from Calibre? The main difference is that the newspaper's table of contents is presented in a way that is much more workable with a touch-screen device. The same applies to magazines that are converted in this way.

WORLD · AFGHAN REFUGEES FORCED TO RETURN HOME

Afghan refugees forced to return home

By <u>Kevin Sieff</u>,

Kabul — During the last stretch of his family's journey home, Esmatullah perched atop a truckload of kitchenware, firewood and furniture, hurtling toward Kabul while the evidence of three decades in exile shifted beneath him.

On either side of the truck, the bazaars grew denser. The buildings became taller and more fortified. American convoys snaked through traffic, heading downtown.

Nearly two days after leaving their home in Pakistan, Esmatullah and his 22 relatives had made it to Afghanistan's capital, after 30 years as refugees. They looked out at their country. They tried not to panic.

The uncertainty shrouding Afghanistan's future has prompted thousands of Afghans to <u>seek an escape route</u> — foreign visa applications, asylum pleas, long journeys across the border. But every day, families swim against that current, returning to Afghanistan after years

Figure 106: The article presentation in a converted newspaper.

eBooks, Calibre, and the Kindle

Believe it or not, there's more to the story. You can manage eBooks—downloaded from Amazon and elsewhere—using Calibre.

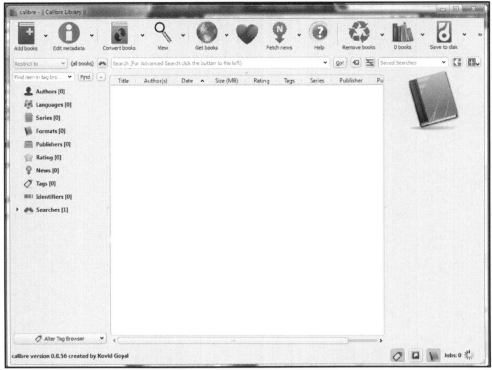

Figure 107: Calibre's main screen

In **Figure 103**, I haven't added my eBooks to the collection yet, so the middle of the screen is blank. There are many ways you can add books to your library. By default, they're sent to the **Calibre Library** folder.

The **Add Books** icon appears at the upper left. Select it, and you'll see the options shown in **Figure 104**.

Add books from a single directory	A
Add books from directories, including sub-directories (One book per directory, assumes every ebook file is the same book in a different format)	
Add books from directories, including sub directories (Multiple books per directory, assumes every ebook file is a different book)	
Add Empty book. (Book entry with no formats)	Ctrl+Shift+E
Add from ISBN	
Add files to selected book records	Shift+A
Control the adding of books	

Figure 108: The Add Books dialog

There are quite a few options here, but we'll concentrate adding one book to the library in a format that Kindle just doesn't like.

In this case, I'm going to add a book that's stored in the EPUB format—a popular one on many sites—but that I want to read on my Amazon Kindle Fire in the native Kindle AZW or MOBI format.

To start, click on "**Add books from a single directory**" and browse to the directory that you want. In **Figure 105**, I've chosen the book "pg1062.epub" which is actually The Raven by Edgar Allen Poe, which I have in the EPUB format that the Kindle will not read. I downloaded it from Project Gutenberg, a site that has plenty of public domain eBooks to choose from and which will be discussed in **Chapter 12**.

Documents library
New folder

Arrange by: Folder ▾

Name	Date modified	Type
Wednesday	6/20/2012 7:59 PM	File folder
Bauhaus - The Sky's Gone Out - 256K CBR MP3 [Kronstadt77]	6/19/2012 12:03 PM	File folder
Blue Jungle _Baby Don't Cry_	6/19/2012 11:47 AM	File folder
pg1062.epub	6/21/2012 4:31 PM	EPUB File

name: pg1062.epub

Books (*.lrf *.rar *.zip *.rtf *.lit *. ▾

Open ▾   Cancel

Figure 109: Choosing a book to import.

In **Figure 106**, you can see that the book has been added to my **Calibre Library**. Notice that even the cover art came over with the import, as did the description and other metatag information. This is one of the handiest features with the Calibre program. I'll change it to more suitable cover art and change the metatags during the conversion process so that they're more descriptive and accurate.

Figure 110: The EBook from Project Gutenberg now appears in My Library.

Before I dump this to my Kindle Fire, I have to convert it. Fortunately, Calibre makes that very easy to do.

Highlight the title and select the "**Covert Books**" icon and then select "**Convert individually**", as shown in **Figure 107** below.

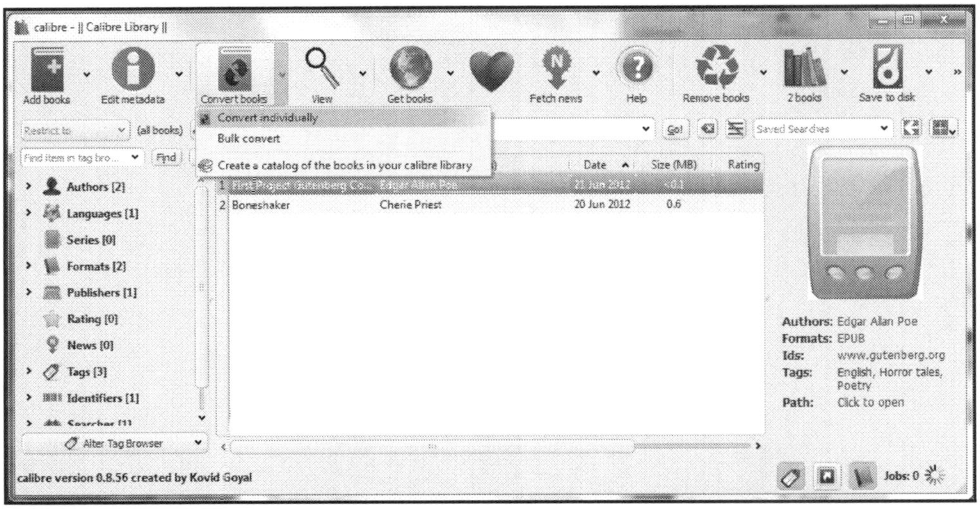

Figure 111: Getting Ready to Covert

Once you select "**Convert individually**", the screen pictured in **Figure 108** will appear.

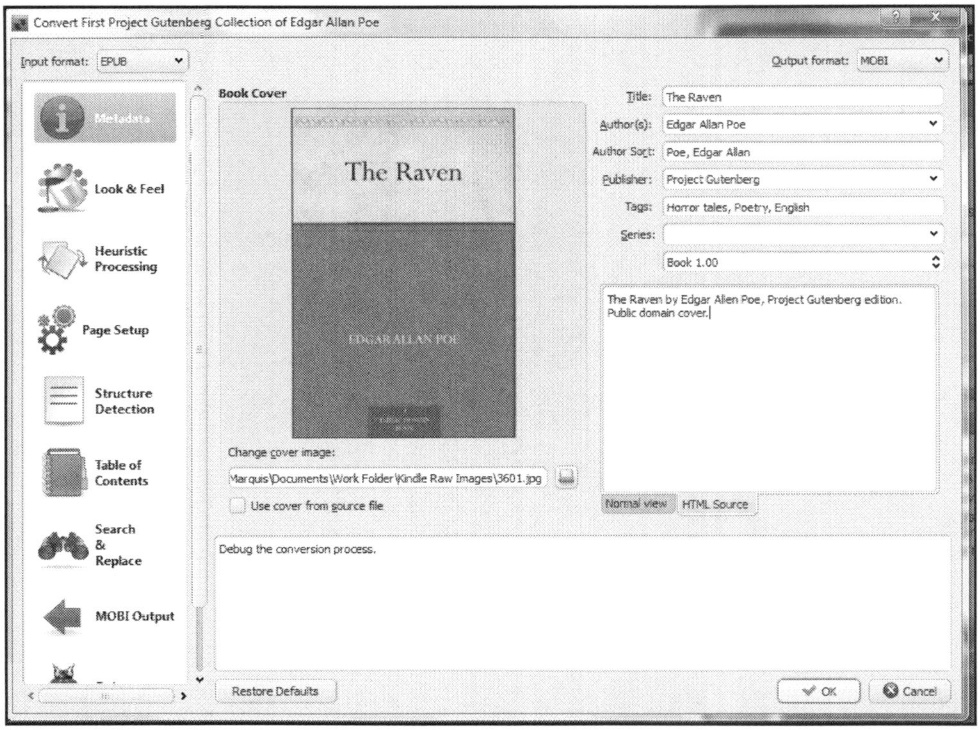

Figure 112: The Convert screen

Take a look at the options available. The **Metadata** selection controls the description, publisher credit and other information associated with the book. Be sure to fill these out if they're not filled out already. They're important organizational tools.

You can also change the cover image, which I've done using a public domain cover that I downloaded. I could technically use any image I wanted, however, as long as it didn't violate anyone's copyright. You can change the **Look and Feel** of the output, which alters the text formatting, and more. One thing that Calibre does very well is give you options!

Because this book needs to be readable on the Kindle Fire, we'll go with the MOBI format, which you can see in the upper right-most dropdown list on **Figure 108**.

The next screen does not show up automatically. Click "**Jobs**" under the main Calibre screen to see it. It shows you the progress of the conversion.

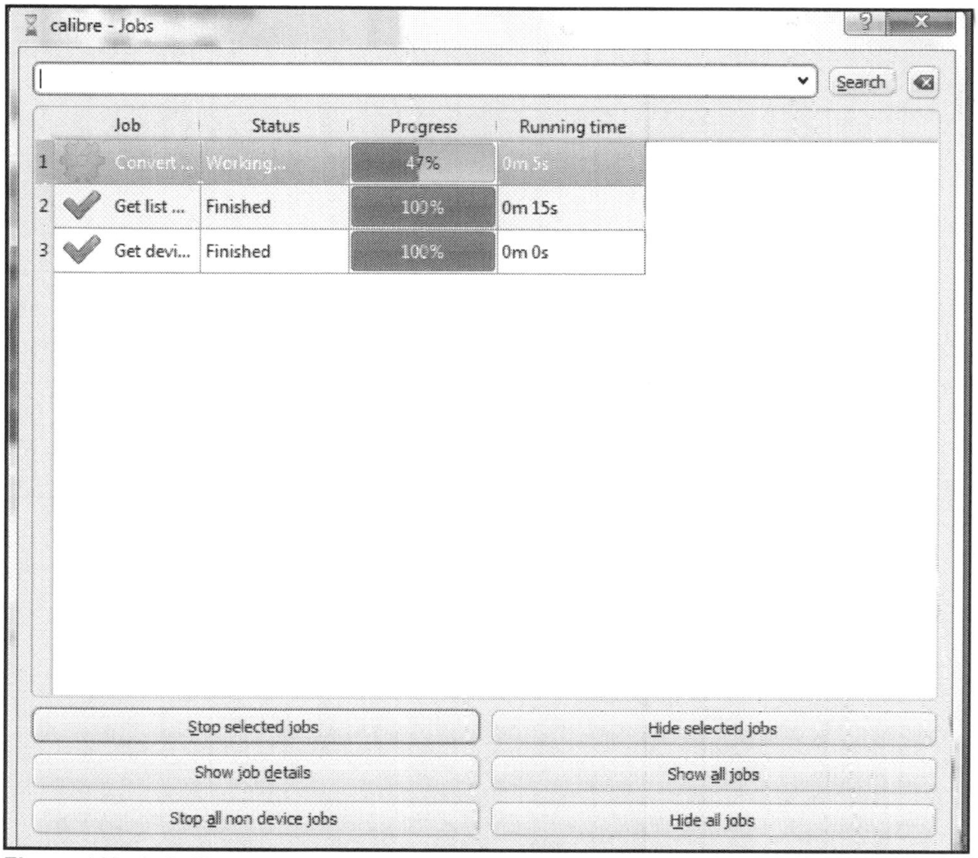

Figure 113: A Calibre conversion in progress.

TIP: You can convert more than one file at once, but it takes a lot of time. If you're going to do so, you might want to get a cup of coffee, order a pizza or do something else to pass the time. If you have a slow computer, consider making your own pizza from scratch!

Now, the file has been converted to the MOBI format, which the Kindle Fire will be entirely happy with, but we have to move it over to the Kindle Fire device, of course.

Select, "**Send to Device**" from the top menu on the main screen. It will pick the device that you set up during the **Welcome Wizard**. Because the Kindle Fire doesn't take an SD card, you can just choose "**Send to main memory**" from the dropdown list. If you did have a device with additional onboard storage, Calibre would give you the option to send it to that storage.

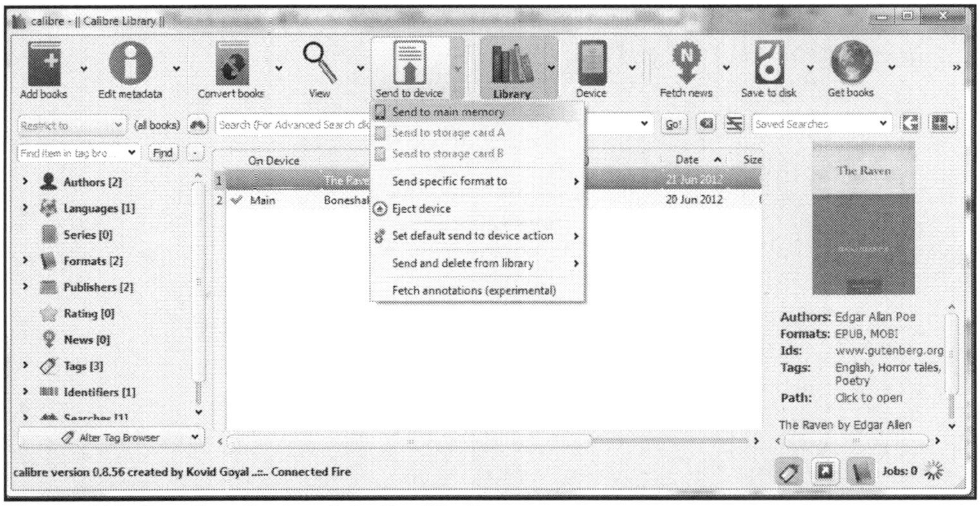

Figure 114: Sending the book to the Kindle.

When the book has been sent, you'll see the listing for it under the "On Device" heading change, as shown in **Figure 111**.

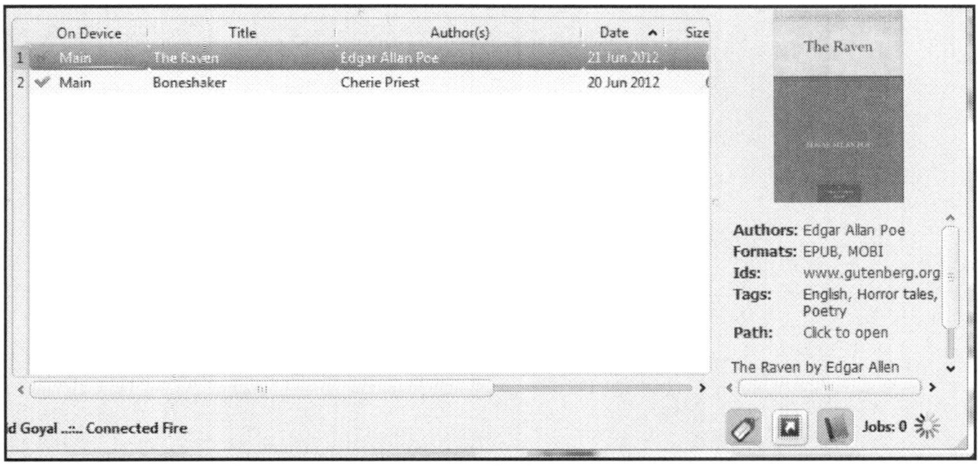

Figure 115: The book now appears on my device.

If I go to my **Books** library on my Kindle Fire and look under the titles available on my device, it shows right up, as pictured in **Figure 112!**

Figure 116: The Raven, Converted to a New Format.

This is only one of the functions that Calibre offers you. It's an amazingly powerful program. We'll explore it more, but be aware that this is going to be one of your most important resources for getting free books off of the Internet. The sites that offer public domain works sometimes don't have them in a format that the Kindle reads. In the future, of course, a format may come along that is incompatible with your Kindle books. Instead of having to buy them in a new format, you'll just be able to convert them!

Briefly: For the love of Calibre

Calibre is the invention of a developer named Kovid Goyal. Though he started the program, it now has many different contributors that keep adding to it, improving it and developing it in new and creative ways. It's a labor of love, and the program is released under the GPL license, which means that it's free for everyone to use as much as they want.

Donations are accepted for this program, so I encourage you to contribute if you benefit from it as I have. Visit http://calibre-ebook.com.

Let's go shopping!

The Kindle Fire makes it easy to go shopping at Amazon, and Calibre makes it easy to go shopping everywhere else. Because it can convert eBooks to different formats, that means that you can hit Amazon, Barnes & Noble, Borders, Project Gutenberg or any other site out there and purchase and download books without worrying about the format.

Click on the "**Get books**" icon on the top of the screen. Because I also have Cherie Priest's book "Boneshaker" on my Calibre and Kindle, I'll get the option to "Search this author," which I'll do.

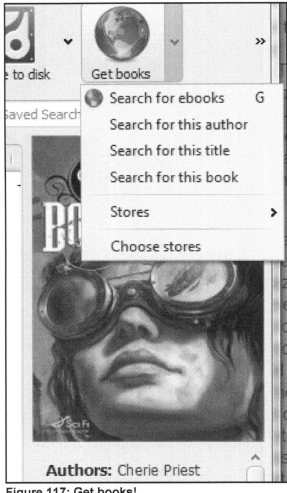

Figure 117: Get books!

If I wanted to, however, I could search for any book using the "**Search for eBooks**" option. I found The Raven using that search function.

The following search dialog will come up. Along the left hand side of the dialog, pictured in **Figure 114**, you'll see options for which stores to search. You can check or uncheck them according to your liking.

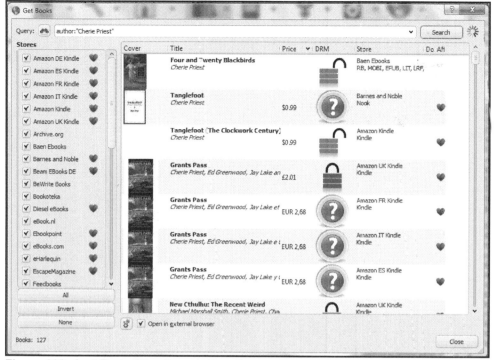

Figure 118: Just Part of the Search Results.

Notice the locks that appear next to some of the listings. This indicates whether the book has DRM (Digital Rights Management or copy prevention). This doesn't mean that you cannot move them from device to device, but you need an additional program to do it. It's called Adobe Digital Editions, which you should have already for downloading books from your public library. Adobe Digital Editions allows you to authorize your eReader, which allows the publisher to manage the DRM properly.

Briefly: The Pirate Code

Piracy, to put it in the simplest terms, means violating someone's copyright by selling, showing or distributing their works in a way that's against the law. For instance, if you remember what it says at the beginning of DVDs and Blu-ray discs, it's essentially that you can play the movie you bought for friends and family but that you cannot charge admission to a showing of that film. It's a violation of your license to do so. Do not use tools to remove DRM restrictions from eBooks. Never make copies of an eBook and distribute them, even for free. That is exactly the definition of piracy. Notice that you have the option of buying books with and without DRM restrictions in **Figure 114**. Just get the DRM-free version or make sure you have Adobe Digital Editions so that you can transfer it properly, if you need to.

Clicking on any of the links in the search results will take you to the appropriate page where you can buy the book. This is an amazing feature, when you think about it. Amazon has just about everything in the way of books, of course, but there are always those books that they don't have and you can search other stores to find them if you need to.

The search feature also searches public domain sources for books. Sort the books by price or by DRM status to get to the public domain versions, if one is available.

Exploring Calibre Further

Calibre has numerous other features. The ways you can use it to enhance your experience using your Kindle Fire are many and, doubtless, you'll find your own ways of using it to make your experience with eBooks, new sources and other media much more enjoyable.

You'll find plenty of documentation and technical information for this program located at http://manual.calibre-ebook.com/. The online manual will let you explore the other functions of this program.

If you don't feel like wading through the online technical documentation, there is an intro video that gives you a nice overview of some of the features discussed in this chapter and more located on the Calibre homepage.

Kindlefeeder

Another popular third-party Kindle service is Kindlefeeder.com. Like Calibre, it enables you to send content that appears on the Internet to your Kindle via email. I suppose it's a bit more easy-to-use at first, but doesn't have the range of Calibre.

11 ▶ ACCESSORIES FOR YOUR KINDLE FIRE

When you first opened the package for your Kindle Fire, you were likely enchanted by what you saw. What Amazon managed to do with this device is to provide a viable tablet computer that provides a lot of punch for a very low price. That being said, the money you paid for your Kindle Fire is nothing to sneeze at.

Some Kindle Fire accessories enhance your experience by protecting your device from harm. Others simply make it more convenient to use in one way or another. In this chapter, we'll take a look at some of the accessories available for this device that make it more fun, that protect it from damage and that expand its capabilities.

The basics

The basic items you need for your Kindle Fire shouldn't really be considered accessories. These are items that you must have if you want your device to last, so we'll list them separately for convenience's sake. You need the following accessories for your Kindle Fire:

- Screen protectors
- A wall-socket charger
- A Mini-USB cord

Screen protectors will generally be available in two different types. There are screen protectors that will dull the display a bit, but produce less glare when you're reading in bright light. These are referred to as matte protectors. There are also protectors that are designed to emphasize the color of your screen—or at least not to mute it—and these are good options if you want to make sure the Kindle Fire looks as brilliant as possible!

These three are givens. Now, let's get to the fun stuff!

TIP: The Amazon Kindle Fire is an exceptionally popular device. Remember that there are far more choices than Amazon where you can shop for accessories. If you want to keep your costs low, you might want to go with the Amazon Basics line of accessories, however. These are priced at a very reasonable level and provide you with something you know will work with your device.

Cases

Figure 119: An Amazon Basics case with kickstand feature. Source: Amazon.com.

Cases are must-have accessories but you can choose many different designs and, for that matter, many different price points. You'll want to choose something that fits your lifestyle.

The advantages of having a case are many. They include:

- Protection for your device
- Extra storage space for your library card or other items that go along with your Kindle Fire
- Style: There are many designs available

When you're considering your case, consider the following aspects of any one that you choose.

Kickstand

Some cases come with modifications that allow you to prop your device up so that you can read it without holding it in your hand. This is great for when you want to watch movies or for when you hook your device up to your speakers so that you can listen to music.

Make sure that the case you choose is high quality. If it's a low quality one, you may find that your Kindle ends up falling over because of a low quality stand.

Pockets

Consider the construction of the device and the amount of padding on the pocket. In general, exterior pockets are better than interior ones. Remember that the cover will close on your device and you don't want anything that might scratch up the screen or otherwise damage it coming into contact with the Kindle Fire.

Materials

When you're reading your Kindle Fire, you're going to be holding it in your hands for a long time. Some people don't like the feel of artificial materials. Some of the really cheap cases out there use plastic and vinyl in their construction and, for some users, this may be very unpleasant. Soft leather or fabric cases are generally very comfortable and, of course, they provide excellent grip, which will prevent you from dropping the device.

Attachments

You'll see cases out there for every type of eReader device. Remember that their principal differentiating characteristic is the way the device is secured into the case. A case for a Kindle Fire will not fit a regular Kindle, for example, so you'll need cases that are specifically made for the Kindle Fire.

Pouches, Envelopes and Sleeves

These are cases into which the Kindle Fire slides but which do not hold the device in place. This means that your Kindle Fire is unprotected when you take it out of the case. These are great for additional protection but your Kindle Fire really should be kept in a case.

Speakers and headphones

There are many different choices out there for audio accessories that go along with your Kindle Fire. Remember that they need a 1/8" plug to connect to your Kindle Fire. As long as they have that, you can choose from any of the following.

Speakers

Speakers come in many shapes and sizes. You can buy small speakers that will fit on your desktop or you can connect to full-fledged 5-speaker systems that allow you to experience the highest quality sound; it's up to you.

One thing you may want to consider is the fact that your Kindle Fire can easily become your new entertainment system. If you want to upgrade your stereo, a high-end set of speakers combined with a Kindle Fire make a great combination!

TIP: Speakers that are advertised as being portable and that are very small usually give lacking sound reproduction. They're fine for use on your desktop, but consider getting headphones instead.

Headphones

Headphones come in models that range from cheap, low- to moderate-quality devices to very expensive models that are intended for DJs and other professionals. You get what you pay for, as always. Some headphones come with their own volume controls, which can be handy if you just want to kick back and listen to music without interacting with your device any more than necessary.

Ear Buds

Ear buds are small speakers that sit directly in your ear canal. They're convenient for their size but their audio quality is usually far less impressive than you'd get out of headphones. For portability, however, they're hard to beat.

TIP: Unless you're a serous audiophile, look in the midrange of prices for speakers and headphones. These should be good enough for most people and, in reality, even a basic set of computer speakers with a subwoofer gives great sound. If you happen to be an apartment dweller, you're probably going to annoy the neighbors if you go for something too powerful, anyway, so concentrate on clarity and price point rather than on raw volume and wattage.

Stylus

The screen on your Kindle Fire is what's called a capacitive touch-screen. The actual workings of it are pretty technical but the technology has some drawbacks. If it's a chilly day and you're wearing gloves, for instance, you won't be able to manipulate the screen without taking them off. A stylus gives you a tool specifically designed to work the Kindle's screen.

There are many different styles of styluses out there. Some of them have additional features, such as a built-in pen or laser pointer.

Styluses make it easier to work the keyboard if you have large fingers, as well, so you may want to consider one of these devices if the on-screen keyboard is frustrating for you. Styluses usually cost between $10 and $20.

TIP: If you're getting a stylus, look for a case with a built in holder for one. It makes it easier to carry around and ensures that you don't lose it.

Figure 120: An inexpensive stylus from Amazon. Source: Amazon.com.

Stands

Stands provide you with a way to prop up your Kindle Fire to watch videos and for other purposes without using a case. Some people prefer them, particularly if they tend not to take their Kindle with them when they go out of the house. If you just want something to hold your Kindle up so you can see it easily, these are good options.

Figure 121: An Amazon Basics stand for Kindle Fire. Source: Amazon.com

12 ▶ OODLES MORE FREE CONTENT FOR YOUR KINDLE

Finding free content for your Kindle Fire isn't difficult. In fact, you'll find that there are plenty of sites out there—including Amazon itself—offering free content of one type or another. These sites may offer a variety of different types of content, from video to audio to books. While you're exploring them, you'll want to avoid illegal pirate sites.

Recognizing illegal content

We touched on illegal content previously but when you're specifically looking for free content, it's imperative that you understand how illegal sites work and how to recognize them. Copyright infringement can turn into a very big deal for people who commit this crime, whether or not they know they're doing it at the time. Here are a few of the red flags to watch out for.

Movies currently in theaters

You can sometimes watch movies online that are still running in theaters, but almost never for free. Amazon's streaming video content, for instance, is fully licensed by the film studios and the company has permission to charge you to watch it. You'll notice that new releases currently in theaters are almost never among the selections. Most of the time, if you see a movie that's currently in theaters on a site that you've never heard of, it's a pirated copy.

Current books offered as free PDF downloads

One of the most common ways that people pirate eBooks is to strip the DRM anti-copying protection off of them, then upload them to peer-to-peer networks. If you know a book is currently selling in eBook form, then a free version is unlikely to be legitimate.

Amazon and other sites, however, do offer samples of books quite frequently. These usually consist of the cover, the table of contents and a few pages that give you an idea of what the author's writing style is like. A free chapter is not too uncommon, either.

Bundled books

Sometimes, you might run across a compressed file containing a large number of eBooks; sometimes these archives contain hundreds of books. These are almost always pirate files. Be sure not to download them. If you consider for a moment that eBooks usually range around $10 a piece, downloading a file containing 100 pirated eBooks equates to $1,000 worth of piracy. That's certainly enough to get you in hot water!

Legal worries might be only part of the problem with illegitimate content. Sometimes the stuff includes a computer virus or malware.

Now, for the good news: There is actually a ton of free content out there that you can download for your Kindle Fire and, better yet, the majority of it is entirely legal.

Adobe Digital Editions

Adobe Digital Editions is a software package many folks use to help borrow eBooks from the library. If you haven't downloaded it yet, you may want to consider doing so now. It allows you to make sure you're in-line with DRM requirements and it's free. Without it, some sites will not let you download free content. Here's how to get it:

Visit http://www.adobe.com/products/digitaleditions/ and download the installer to get started.

After you install the program, it will automatically manage your purchases and your library loans for you. Notice the two buttons on the top left-hand side of the screen in Figure 119. These allow you to switch between **Library View** and **Reading View**. If you want to read your downloaded documents right on your computer, you can do so by clicking on the Reading View icon.

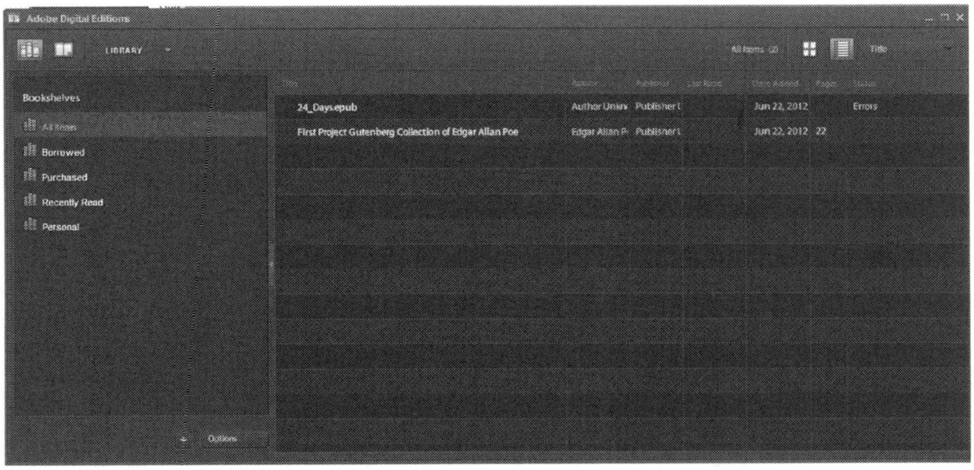

Figure 122: The Adobe Digital Editions home-screen.

When you purchase books from Amazon, you can just go to http://Amazon.com/myk to manage them. When you get books from a public library or from some other sources, however, you'll have to use Adobe Digital Editions to manage them.

Library Books

Library books will show up automatically in this program when you download them from sources other than Amazon.com. One of the handy things that this program does is put up a banner that lets you know how much time you have remaining on the library loan. The other great thing it does is return the book for you.

What do you mean 'Return?'

With an eBook, there's no physical object that you borrow or return. You're simply given a license that allows you to read the eBook for however long you check it out. At the end of that licensing term, the content is no longer accessible to you.

The book will, however, show up in your **Library**. If you click on it, you'll get a dialogue telling you the item is expired. To get it out of your **Library**:

1. Click the arrow to the left of the title
2. Select "**Delete Item**"
3. The item will be removed from your **Library**

Public Domain books

Many older popular books are no longer under copyright, and so they're in the "Public Domain" and usually available free in eBook formats. For instance, the works of Edgar Allen Poe, Mary Shelly, Jane Austin and Charlotte Bronte were written so long ago, nobody owns the rights anymore. There is a caveat here, however.

If you buy a specific publisher's edition of a public domain work, that edition is copyrighted. The edition likely has unique material in it that does fall under the copyright protection of the publisher and, therefore, it cannot be reproduced in full. To put it in shorthand terms: You can reproduce "The Raven" all you want, but you cannot reproduce a copyrighted analysis of "The Raven" included in a printing of the poem.

There are several sites that offer public domain books. The most well-known is likely Project Gutenberg, located at http://www.gutenberg.org/.

Exploring Project Gutenberg

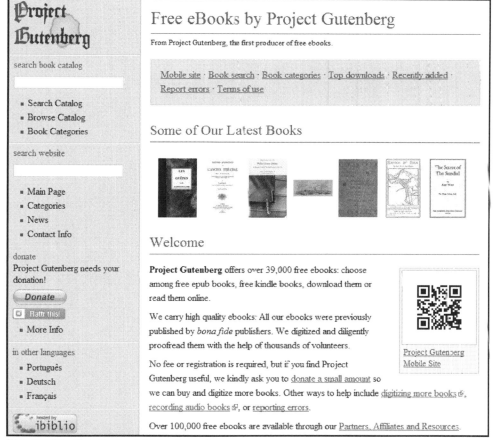

Figure 123: The Project Gutenberg homepage

Figure 123 shows the Project Gutenberg homepage. The left navigation menu gives you access to the site's entire book catalog. You can choose to **Search Catalog**, **Browse Catalog** or you can view **Book Categories**.

Let's search for a well-known suspense story, "The Turn of the Screw" by Henry James. Here is the result from Project Gutenberg:

Figure 124: Search results for 'Turn of the Screw' at Project Gutenberg.

Notice that, on the right of the page, there are two results listed. The first is a link to all the eBook versions of The Turn of the Screw. The one below it is a link to the audio version of the story. Project Gutenberg has a lot of audio books that are public domain and that are read by volunteers. If you want to stock up on audio books for a long trip, this is a good place to do it!

Let's click on the like to the eBook version of The Turn of the Screw.

Format	Size	Mirror Sites
HTML	263 kB	mirror sites
EPUB (no images)	107 kB	
Kindle (no images)	447 kB	
Plucker	148 kB	
QiOO Mobile	156 kB	
Plain Text UTF-8	247 kB	
More Files...		mirror sites

Figure 125: The eBook Versions of 'The Turn of The Screw.'

Project Gutenberg will typically offer books in a variety of formats. Notice that there are HTML, EPUB, Kindle, PLocker, QiOO Mobile and Plain Text versions of this eBook.

Simply click on the link to download the eBook and save it to your computer. You can either transfer the book to your Kindle Fire manually or you can do so through your Calibre library, which will allow you to assign it a cover and other metadata, as I did with The Raven in **Chapter 10**.

TIP: Project Gutenberg oftentimes offers books with images or without the images. Since you have the Kindle Fire's color display, you'll definitely want to download the version with images.

Amazon free books for Kindle

Earlier in this book, we discussed my website KindleBuffet.com, which lists current eBooks being offered during brief promotional periods. In addition to those books, Amazon offers thousands of classic Public Domain works absolutely free. Unlike the Kindle Buffet selections, these books remain free all year long, and many of them are the same texts available through Project Gutenberg.

Let's do a search for "Bronte". This will bring up books by the Bronte sisters—Ann, Charlotte and Emily—as shown below:

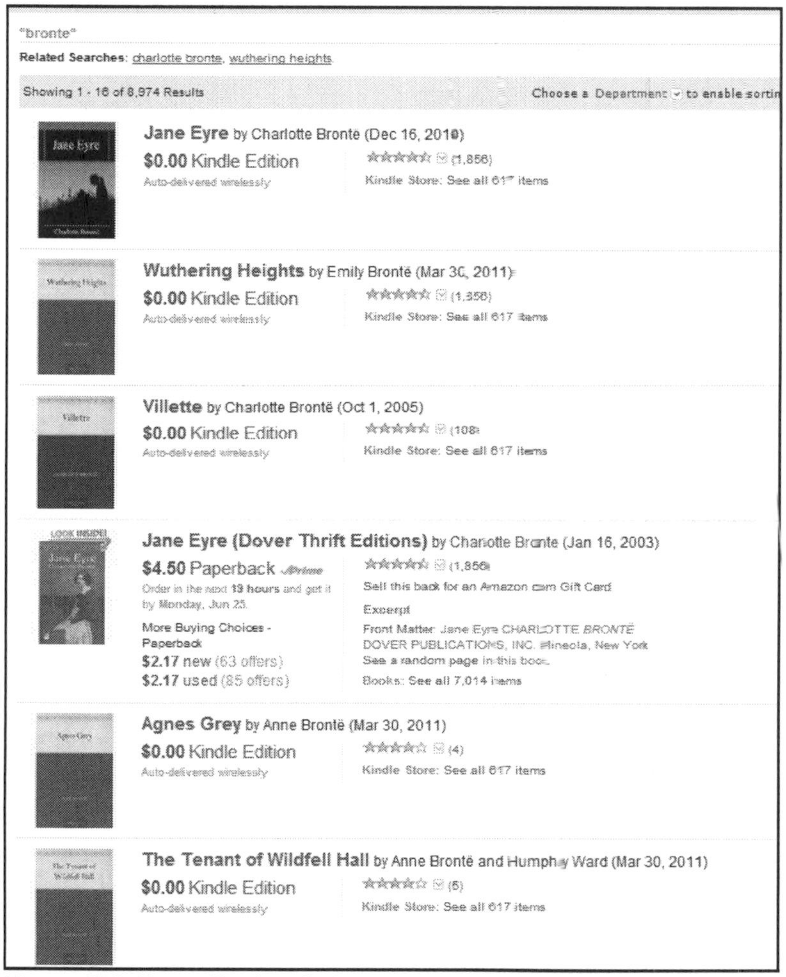

Figure 126: Free eBooks of classic novels by the Bronte sisters.

Notice the books with the generic beige and green covers and the book with the Kindle graphic for a cover. They're all priced at $0.00. These are Public Domain titles, so Amazon lets you download them for free to your Kindle. The beige and green covers appear on several of the books in my library, pictured in **Figure 127**. These are all free—and rather hard-to-find in printed form—books that I got from Amazon.com.

In the image below, King Henry V by Shakespeare, Four Weird Tales by Algernon Blackwood, The Centaur by Algernon Blackwood, The Return by Walter de la Mare and the Raven by Edgar Allen Poe were all free. Amazon has a huge collection available.

Figure 127: My Library showing several free books.

TIP: Many rare and out-of-print books are now available as eBooks from several different sites. If you've been searching for a book that means a lot to you to own—maybe something from your childhood or with similar sentimental value—be sure to check Project Gutenberg and Amazon. It may well be available on one of these sites.

Purchasing free books on Amazon. Even though a particular book might be "free," you'll still need a One-Click payment method at Amazon to download them. You'll get a receipt in your email that will show the purchase but nothing will show up on your credit card or bank statement.

The Kindle Owner's Lending Library

You also have access to the Kindle Owner's Lending Library, a feature that comes if you choose to keep your Amazon Prime subscription. This is very easy to access:

1. Open up your **Books** library and go to **Store**
2. On the right-hand side of the screen, select "**Kindle Owner's Lending Library**"
3. Select a Category
4. Look for books with the Prime logo under them that are proceed at $0.00
5. Tap on the book to select it.
6. Select "**Borrow for Free**"
7. The item will be downloaded to your library.

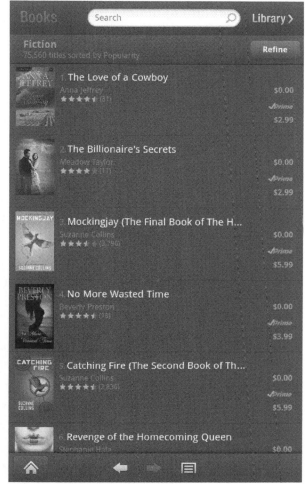

Figure 128: The fiction Kindle Owner's Lending Library.

Books may be returned at any time, but you have to return the book you have before you can borrow another. Go to http://Amazon.com/myk to return a book so that you can borrow another.

Finding free video

We know there's a ton of free video available through your Amazon Prime account, but what if you want to search beyond Amazon? Fortunately, the Kindle Fire gives you plenty of options in this regard.

Because it supports Flash, you can watch video hosted at most sites. For example, you can tune into the original Star Trek series—and many other classic television shows—on CBS.com.

TIP: Network websites oftentimes have many of their classic television shows available for free online. Be sure to check them out! Here are some other resources.

Archive.org

Officially known as the Internet Archive, pictured in Figure 124, Archive.org has a huge collection of Public Domain videos available. The site is free to use. There are government produced clips—the ones from the 50's and 60's being particularly amusing—and there are classic films that have fallen into the public domain. Before you start thinking that all public domain films must be awful, think again! Some of the most well-known and beloved films are in the public domain.

Figure 129: The Internet Archive homepage.

Briefly: You've got that Zombie feeling

While most films and other works enter the Public Domain due to age, this isn't always the case. Currently, "zombies" are among the hottest book, movie, television and video game antagonists in the world. Most of these zombies owe some of their behavior to the zombies in George Romero's cult-classic 1968 film, "Night of the Living Dead". And believe it or not, that film is in the Public Domain. Why? The film distributor neglected to put the copyright notice on the original prints of the film, which rendered the copyright claim invalid, according to the law at the time. The result: You can watch Night of the Living Dead on the Internet Archive and other Public Domain sites.

Google Video/YouTube

YouTube.com is one of the best sites for free video of all types. Because much of it is user-generated, you don't have to worry about copyright issues. YouTube is a great place to go if you want to see:

- Viral Videos

- Movie Trailers
- Classic TV Commercials
- Independent News
- Major News Organization Videos
- Much More

You can use the search engine at http://google.com/video to search the entire YouTube site. Remember that YouTube has plenty of public domain movies, as well.

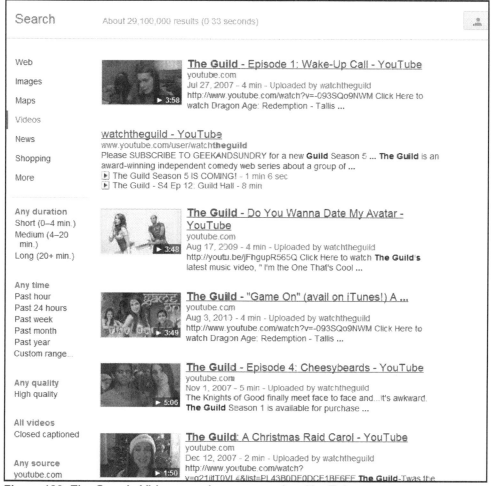

Figure 130: The Google Video search page searches YouTube.

TIP: If you cannot see YouTube videos, be sure you have Flash enabled on your Kindle Fire's browser settings.

Netflix

Even though the Kindle Fire is tied to the Amazon.com webpage, you can still use it to view movies from other sources. If you have a Netflix account, you can watch movies instantly by using the Netflix app available in the App store. (The app is free but Netflix charges a monthly membership fee.)

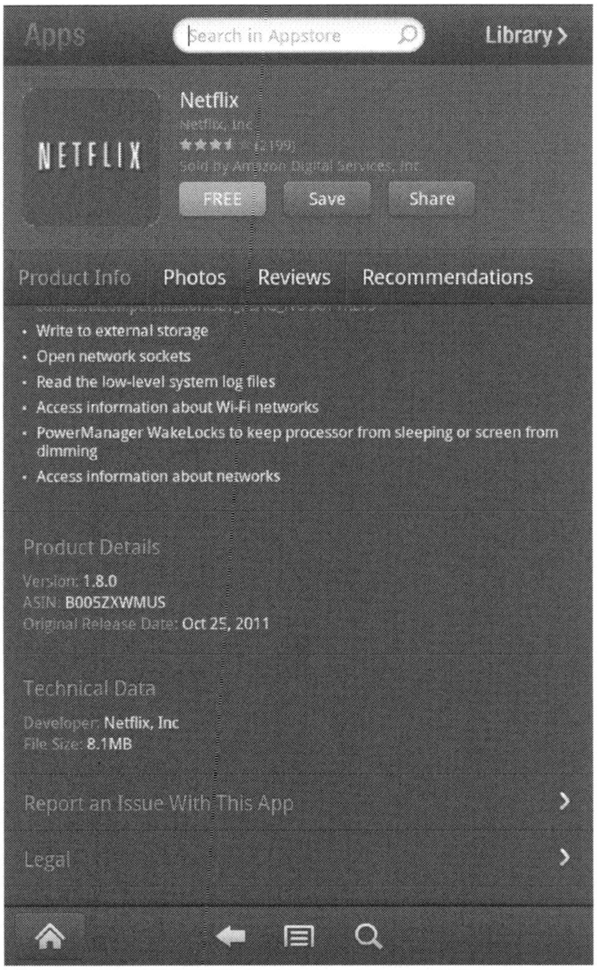

Figure 131: Downloading the Netflix app for Kindle Fire.

Getting free apps

The most important thing to remember about downloading apps outside Amazon's App store is that they can pose a danger to your Kindle Fire. Some of them are poorly designed and may cause issues with the operating system, while some are downright malicious.

The safest place for you to download apps, by far, is the **App** store on Amazon. If you want some other options, however, here are some sites to consider.

GetJar

GetJar has plenty of great apps that will work with your Amazon Kindle Fire. Your Kindle Fire is on the Android operating system and that's what this site specializes in. Many of the apps are free, as you can see in **Figure 132**. They also allow you to break away from Amazon's control of your device. Amazon did a good job with the device, of course, but you paid for a tablet computer and should be able to use it to its fullest! The site is located at http://www.getjar.com/.

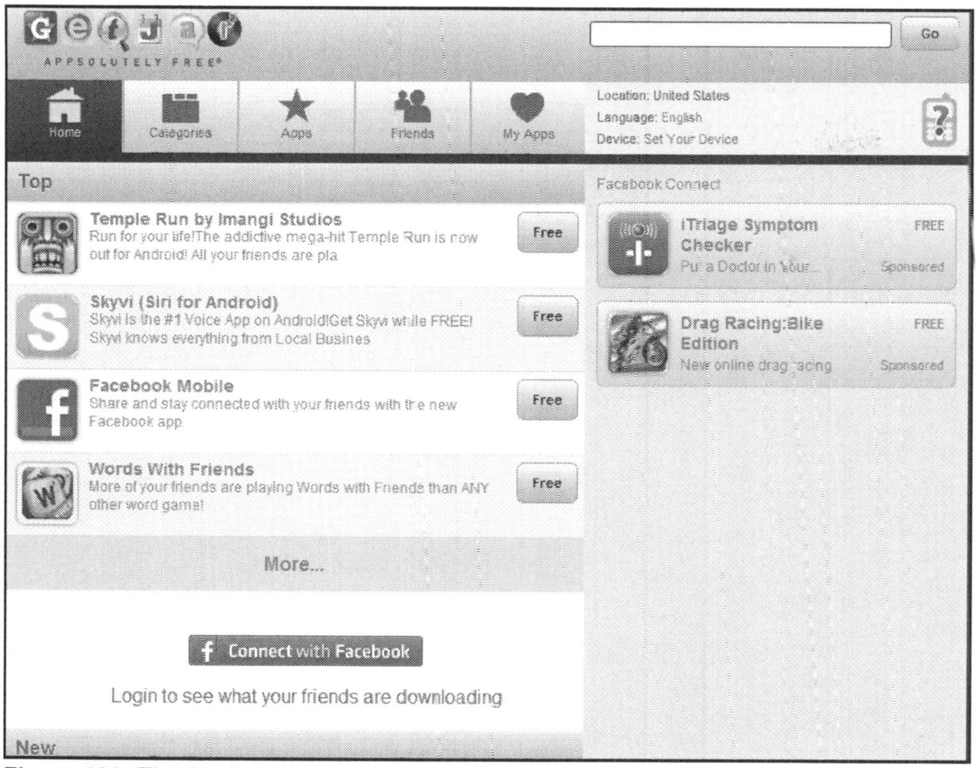

Figure 132: The GetJar Homepage.

SlideMe

SlideMe is another Android app store that offers you more than what you could get at Amazon's app store. They have plenty of games and other free applications that you can choose from. Remember to check the community reviews of applications before you download them; it can prevent you from downloading a dud!

Figure 133: The SlideMe Homepage.

OnlyAndroid

OnlyAndroid has a lot of great applications that you can choose from. You'll find both paid and free applications at this site. As a tip, paid applications are usually a bit safer and sometimes come with support options that can be a big help if you get confused while you're using them. Check them out at http://onlyandroid.mobihand.com/.

Figure 134: OnlyAndroid's Homepage.

Google Play

If there's an official Android app homepage, this is it. Google Play is the largest repository for apps that will work with your Android. There are some real caveats to keep in mind with this site, however.

First, there have been issues with bad apps being uploaded to the site. The Google Play store is popular precisely because it lacks the overly-restrictive nature of competitors such as the Apple iPhone app store. It's pretty much a free for all as far as uploading apps goes, but the requirements have been tightened somewhat.

Second, many of these apps are going to be for cellular phones specifically. Remember that your Kindle Fire does not have any telephone capabilities built into it, so you'll find that some of these apps will really not make any sense at all on your Kindle. Some can be customized, such as the Go Launcher EX app that was discussed in **Chapter 9**.

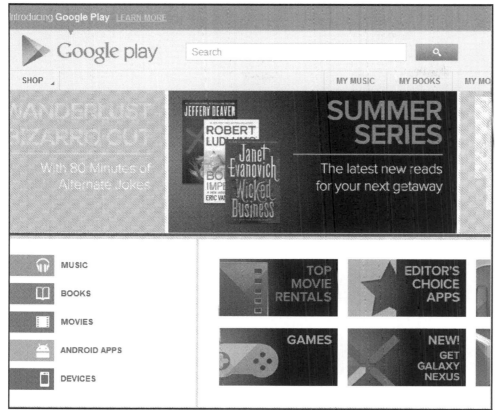

Figure 135: Google Play homepage

Downloading apps outside Amazon

The Google Play store is extremely difficult where installing apps is concerned. You have to either "root" your device—which may void any warranties you have on it—or you have to side load the app by downloading the APK over Mini USB. If that sounds like a foreign language to you, you may just want to skip using the Google Play store altogether. With the other apps, however, it's pretty easy.

Select to install the app on the site that applies by using your web browser, shown in **Figure 136**.

Figure 136: GetJar.com, click Download to Get the App Files.

When the download completes, check your notification area at the top of your screen, shown in **Figure 137**.

Tap on whatever APK file applies, go through the wizard and your app will install. That's all there is to it. Google Play is really the only site that's hard to work with.

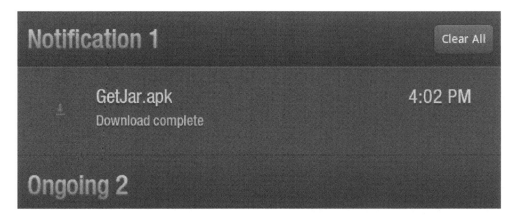

Remember, you have to set your browser up to allow third-party installations to download apps outside Amazon.

Index

20611626R00082

Made in the USA
Lexington, KY
12 February 2013